CLYBOURNE PARK

BY **BRUCE NORRIS**

DRAMATISTS
PLAY SERVICE
INC.

CLYBOURNE PARK
Copyright © 2012, Bruce Norris

All Rights Reserved

SPECIAL NOTE

For Frances Watson

CLYBOURNE PARK was produced on Broadway by Jujamcyn Theaters at the Walter Kerr Theatre on April 19, 2012. It was directed by Pam MacKinnon; the set design was by Daniel Ostling; the costume design was by Ilona Somogyi; the lighting design was by Allen Lee Hughes; the sound design was by John Gromada; the hair and wig design were by Charles LaPonte; and the stage manager was C. A. Clark. The cast was as follows:

RUSS/DAN .... Frank Wood
BEV/KATHY .... Christina Kirk
FRANCINE/LENA .... Crystal A. Dickinson
JIM/TOM/KENNETH .... Brendan Griffin
ALBERT/KEVIN .... Damon Gupton
KARL/STEVE .... Jeremy Shamos
BETSY/LINDSEY .... Annie Parisse

The World Premiere of CLYBOURNE PARK was produced Off-Broadway by Playwrights Horizons in 2010.

CHARACTERS

Act One (1959)

RUSS (white, late 40s)

BEV (married to Russ; white, 40s)

FRANCINE (black, 30s)

JIM (white, late 20s)

ALBERT (married to Francine; black, 30s)

KARL (white, 30s)

BETSY (married to Karl, late 20s)

Act Two (2009)

TOM (played by the actor who played Jim)

LINDSEY (played by the actor who played Betsy)

KATHY (played by the actor who played Bev)

STEVE (married to Lindsey; played by the actor who played Karl)

LENA (played by the actor who played Francine)

KEVIN (married to Lena; played by the actor who played Albert)

DAN (played by the actor who played Russ)

KENNETH (played by the actor who played Jim)

SETTING

The set is the interior of a modest three-bedroom bungalow, 406 Clybourne Street, in the near northwest of central Chicago. There is a sitting room with front door access, a fireplace with an oak mantelpiece, and a separate dining area with built-in cupboards. At the rear of the dining area, a swinging door leads to a kitchen. A staircase leads up to a second floor, and beneath it, another door leads down to a basement. There is a hallway and a bathroom door as well.

NOTE

In the original production, the actor playing Jim and Tom also played the role of Kenneth. In some subsequent productions a separate actor was hired to play the role of Kenneth alone.

CLYBOURNE PARK

ACT ONE

September 1959. Three o'clock, Saturday afternoon. The house is in disarray. Cardboard boxes are stacked in corners. Some furniture has been removed, shelves emptied. Pictures have been removed from the walls and carpets have been rolled and stood on end. Not far from the fireplace, Russ sits alone reading a copy of National Geographic. *He is dressed in pajama top and chinos, socks, no shoes. On a table next to him sits a carton of ice cream into which, from time to time, he dips a spoon. Music plays softly on a radio next to him.*

After some time, Bev descends the stairs carrying linens to place in a cardboard box. As she packs, she stops to look at Russ.

BEV. You're not going to eat all of that, are you? *(He turns down the radio.)*
RUSS. *(With his mouth full.)* Whaddya say?
BEV. What ice cream is that?
RUSS. Um. *(Looks at the carton.)* Neapolitan.
BEV. Well, don't feel compelled to eat that.
RUSS. *(Shrugs, barely audible.)* Going to waste. *(He turns the radio back up and Francine enters from the kitchen, wearing a maid's uniform. Russ remains in the foreground as Bev joins her.)*
FRANCINE. *(To Bev.)* So, if it's all right I'm just going to put these candlesticks here in the big box with the utensils.
BEV. That is what I would do, yes, but you do mean to wrap them first?
FRANCINE. Oh, yes ma'am.

BEV. Oh. Now: Francine: I was wondering about this chafing dish, which we have practically never used.

FRANCINE. Yes, ma'am.

BEV. Do you own one of these yourself?

FRANCINE. No, I sure don't.

BEV. Because I do love to entertain though for the life of me I can't remember the last time we did. But still, it does seem a shame to give it away because it's just such a nice thing, isn't it?

FRANCINE. Oh, yes it is.

BEV. And it just looks so lonely sitting there in the cupboard *so*: I was wondering if this might be the sort of thing that would be useful to you?

FRANCINE. Ohhhh, thank you, I couldn't take that.

BEV. *(Re: chafing dish.)* See how sad he looks?

FRANCINE. You don't want to be giving that to me.

BEV. Well, nonetheless I'm offering.

FRANCINE. No, I don't think I should.

BEV. Well, you think about it.

FRANCINE. But thank you for offering.

BEV. You think about it and let me know.

FRANCINE. Yes, ma'am.

BEV. And do put some paper around those.

FRANCINE. Yes, ma'am. *(Francine goes into kitchen. Bev returns with more to pack, passing Russ.)*

BEV. That's a funny word, isn't it? Neapolitan.

RUSS. *(Turns off radio.)* Funny what way?

BEV. What do you suppose is the origin of that?

RUSS. Uhhh … Naples, I imagine.

BEV. *Naples?*

RUSS. City of Naples?

BEV. Noooo.

RUSS. Of or pertaining to.

BEV. That would not be my first guess.

RUSS. Yup.

BEV. *I* would think it had something to do with *neo*, as in something *new*, and then there's the *-politan* part which to me would suggest a *city*, like *metropolitan*.

RUSS. Could be.

BEV. Meaning *new city* or something to that effect.

RUSS. *(Shrugs.)* Told you what *I* think.

BEV. Because a person from Naples, I mean they wouldn't be called, well, not *Napoleon*, obviously. I guess that was already taken! *(Laughs, then serious.)* On the other hand, you *do* say *Italian*. But *cities*, though, and specifically ones that end in *S*, because there must be a rule of some sort, don't you think? Help me think of a city other than *Naples* that also ends in S? *(Pause.)*

RUSS. Uhhh —

BEV. Oh fiddle. Um.

RUSS. Des Moines.

BEV. Not a *silent* S.

RUSS. Brussels.

BEV. All right. There you go. And how do we refer to them?

RUSS. Belgians.

BEV. But, the people from the *city*.

RUSS. Never *met* anyone from Brussels.

BEV. But there has to be a word.

RUSS. Look it up.

BEV. Where?

RUSS. Dictionary?

BEV. But it's not going to say this is the capital of Belgium and by the way the people who live there are called —

RUSS. Give Sally a call.

BEV. She won't know that.

RUSS. She and Ray went to Paris.

BEV. So?

RUSS. *Close* to Brussels.

BEV. Sally never knows those sorts of things.

RUSS. Oh. Oh.

BEV. What?

RUSS. Parisians.

BEV. What about them? *(Francine returns with more packing.)*

RUSS. Paris ends in S.

BEV. But — It's not *Brusselsians*.

RUSS. Or Nice.

BEV. I'm serious.

RUSS. Got the "S" *sound*.

BEV. But not *Nicians*. Like *Grecians*.

RUSS. No, no. *Niçoise*.

BEV. I know that, but —

RUSS. Know that salad your sister makes?

9

BEV. But that's *French*.

RUSS. It's a French *city*.

BEV. I understand, but, I'm saying how would we say, in *Eng* — ? Well, now I don't remember the original question.

RUSS. Brussels.

BEV. No no.

RUSS. Des Moines?

BEV. *No.*

RUSS. Naples.

BEV. *Naples.* And I don't think *Neapolitan.* How would that become *Neapolitan*?

RUSS. Muscovites.

BEV. What?

RUSS. People from Moscow.

BEV. Well, I give up, because that's just *peculiar*.

RUSS. *(Chuckles at the word.)* Muscovites.

BEV. *(The same.)* I wonder if they're musky.

RUSS. *(Savoring the sound.)* Musss-covites.

BEV. *(Coming up with one.)* Cairenes!

RUSS. *That* is a strange one.

BEV. I'm telling you, that's what they're called!

RUSS. I'm not disputing.

BEV. But why *Cairenes*?

RUSS. *(Shrugs.)* Dated a girl named *Irene. (Francine exits again.)*

BEV. Or *Congolese*?

RUSS. That, too, is correct.

BEV. So why don't we say *Tongalese*?

RUSS. Or *Mongolese.*

BEV. No, Mongol-*oid.*

RUSS. No no, that's different.

BEV. Oh, you're right.

RUSS. That's uhhh, you know, that's —

BEV. No, I know.

RUSS. *(Tapping his finger on his temple.)* The thing with the —

BEV. *(Doing the same.)* Like the Wheeler boy.

RUSS. Right. The one who —

BEV. Bags the groceries.

RUSS. Right.

BEV. *(Beat, then.)* But that's nice, isn't it, in a way? To know we all have our place.

RUSS. There but for the grace of god.

BEV. Exactly. *(Pause. Russ breaks it with:)*

RUSS. *(Pronouncing grandly, with a sweep of his hand.)* Ulan Bator!

BEV. What?

RUSS. *(An exact repeat.)* Ulan Bator!

BEV. What are you doing?

RUSS. *(Once again.)* Ulan — !

BEV. Stop it. Tell me what you're doing.

RUSS. Capital of Mongolia.

BEV. Well, why would I know that?

RUSS. *(Shrugs.) National Geographic.*

BEV. Oh oh. Did you change the address like I asked you?

RUSS. What do you mean?

BEV. For the *National Geographic.*

RUSS. The address?

BEV. Oh, *Russ!*

RUSS. Me?

BEV. I *asked* you.

RUSS. You did?

BEV. I asked you *fifteen times.*

RUSS. When?

BEV. I said don't forget the change of address for the magazine and you promised me that you would, you promised me *specifically* —

RUSS. *(Overlapping.)* I did it last week.

BEV. *(Continuous.)* — that you would see to it so I — Oh.

RUSS. Pulling your leg.

BEV. I see.

RUSS. *(A gentle imitation.)* Oh *Russ!!*

BEV. Maybe people don't *like* having their leg pulled.

RUSS. I was just — I was — Okay. *(Pause.)*

BEV. And are you going to bring that trunk down from upstairs?

RUSS. Yup.

BEV. Thought you said after lunch.

RUSS. Sort a two-person job.

BEV. And you really want to wear those clothes all day?

RUSS. Hadn't really thought about it. *(A silence passes between them. Russ scratches his elbow.).*

BEV. But you know, you *are* a funny person. I was telling Francine — I ran into Barbara Buckley at Lewis and Coker's and Barbara said that Newland told her a funny joke that you told at Rotary last year.

RUSS. That *I* told?

BEV. About a man with a talking dog?

RUSS. *(Shakes his head.)* Thinking of Ron Lassiter.

BEV. No, It was you.

RUSS. Ron's the one with the jokes.

BEV. You know jokes. You tell jokes.

RUSS. A talking *dog*?

BEV. And Barbara said does Russ not go to Rotary anymore? Apparently they all keep saying where's Russ? *(A beat, then.)* Not that I care one way or the other but it does seem that you used to enjoy going and I don't see why that, of all things, should have to change — *(Russ shifts in his chair. Continuous, quickly.)* — and please don't say *what's the point*, Russ. I hate it when you say that. Because for that matter —

RUSS. *(Overlapping.)* I wasn't going to say —

BEV. *(Continuous.)* — what's the point of *anything* enjoyable, really? — *(Phone rings. Francine enters. Continuous.)* — Why not just sit in a chair all day and wait for the end of the world but *I* don't intend to live the remainder of my life like that and I think you could take notice of the fact that talking that way *frightens* me.

FRANCINE. *(Phone.)* Stoller residence?

RUSS. *(Quietly, to Bev.)* Not trying to frighten you.

FRANCINE. Who may I say is calling, please?

RUSS. *(To Bev, quietly.)* Ulan Bator.

FRANCINE. Excuse me, Miz Stoller?

BEV. Who is it?

FRANCINE. Mister Lindner wanting to talk to you.

RUSS. *(With a groan.)* Ohh for the love of —

BEV. *(To Francine.)* Tell him I'll call him back.

RUSS. Not one thing it's another.

FRANCINE. *(Phone.)* Mister Lindner, she wonders if she can call you back?

BEV. *(Overlapping Francine, to Russ.)* I only mean that people are concerned about you —

RUSS. *(Overlapping.)* Well, what's the *nature* of the concern?

BEV. *(Continuous.)* — and I don't see the point of *spurning* their good intentions.

RUSS. Gee whiz I'm just reading a magazine.

FRANCINE. *(To Bev.)* Says he's calling from a pay phone.

RUSS. *(To Francine.)* Just say we're occupied.

BEV. No, I'll take it, thank you Francine. *(To Russ, as she crosses.)* I'm just repeating what Barbara said. *(Into phone.)* Hello?

RUSS. *(To himself.)* Barely know the woman.

BEV. *(Phone.)* No no no, it's just, we're in a state of disarray, Karl.

RUSS. Somehow I *spurned* her. *(As Francine returns to the kitchen, the front door opens and Jim sticks his head in. He is a youthful minister — wears a clerical collar under his jacket.)*

JIM. Ding dong?

RUSS. *(Seeing Jim, not rising.)* Oh. Uh, hey, Bev?

JIM. May one intrude, he politely asked?

RUSS. *(To Bev.)* Jim's at the door.

BEV. *(Seeing Jim, she mouths silently to him.)* Oh, oh, oh! *Come in!! Come in!! (Into phone.)* Karl, I can't hear what you're saying.

JIM. Russ, my friend, I am crossing the threshold!

RUSS. Hey Jim.

JIM. *(Looking around.)* Holy Toledo Jiminy Christmas.

RUSS. Bev's on the phone.

JIM. Hate to be the one to break it to ya, buddy, but somebody made off with yer stuff!

RUSS. Kinda discombobulated.

BEV. *(Phone.)* Oh, Karl, I don't think so, not today.

JIM. *(To Russ.)* 'S not the big day, is it?

RUSS. *(To Jim.)* No no. Monday.

BEV. *(Phone.)* No, it's just, Russ is a little under the weather.

JIM. Piece of advice. Watch out when you start lifting things. Learned that the hard way last month.

RUSS. *(Preoccupied with Bev.)* Izzat right?

JIM. Ohhhh *yeah.* Judy says Jim, I gotta have me this spinet piano, a task which naturally falls to *me* —

BEV. *(Phone, overlapping.)* Well, if it's absolutely necessary.

JIM. *(Continuous.)* — and there I am with this thing halfway up the front steps and me *underneath.* And of course, it's not the weight, you know. It's the *angle* —

BEV. All right, Karl. *(Hangs up.)*

JIM. *(Continuous.)* — which is why they tell ya to bend the knees.

BEV. *(Re: Jim.)* Well, will you look what the cat dragged in?

RUSS. *(To Bev, re: the phone call.)* What was that about?

JIM. Bev, I am *trying* to bestow the pearls of my wisdom upon this man.

RUSS. *(To Jim.)* No no, I was listening.

BEV. Oh, isn't it just a *jumble* in here, all of this?

JIM. 'S what I was saying to Russ, said somebody cleaned ya out!

RUSS. Not coming here, is he?

BEV. Oh, I don't know. You know Karl.

JIM. Karl Lindner?

RUSS. Bev?

JIM. Ohmigosh. Ya got a look at Betsy lately?

BEV. *(Eyes wide.)* Oh, I *know.*

JIM. Give that girl a *wide berth.*

BEV. Jim, can I get you some iced tea?

RUSS. *(To Bev.)* Maybe call back and ask him to come later.

BEV. It was a pay phone. *(To Jim.)* Oh oh oh oh oh! I know! Now wait. Now Jim: I am going to ask you a question:

JIM. Huh-oh!

BEV. *(To Russ.)* And don't help him. *(To Jim.)* Now: I want you to tell Russ what you think the word *Neapolitan* means.

RUSS. *(To Jim.)* She thought —

BEV. *Shhhhhhh!!!* You're not allowed to say.

JIM. Well, that'd be your basic vanilla, strawb —

BEV. No no. The *derivation.*

RUSS. I *told* her what I th —

BEV. *Shhhhh!!!*

JIM. Uh, think it's *Naples*, isn't it?

BEV. Ohhhhh *phooey.*

JIM. Or *Napoli*, as we like to say. *(Francine enters.)*

BEV. You two are *cheating.* And then — well, Russ's in a funny mood ... he keeps going *(Trying to do what Russ did.)* Oo-lan Ba-tor!

JIM. Whatzat, capital of Nepal?

RUSS. Mongolia.

JIM. Mongolia. So then what's the *Nepalese* — Do ya say *Nepalese*?

BEV. *(Chuckles, slaps Russ's arm.)* I hope it's not Ne-*politan*!

RUSS. Kathmandu.

JIM. *Kathmandu!*

BEV. Oh, well, I don't even know why you two know these things.

FRANCINE. Miz Stoller?

JIM. Knowledge is power, Bev.

BEV. Then I choose to remain *powerless.* *(To Russ.)* Do it again.

RUSS. Do what?

BEV. How you said it.

RUSS. No.

BEV. *Do* it, Russ.

RUSS. No.

BEV. Do it for Jim.

RUSS. Bev?

BEV. Why *not?*

RUSS. Sorry, Jim.

BEV. Why for me but not for him?

RUSS. Well, for one thing, 'cuz it's not *funny.*

FRANCINE. Excuse me, I'm fixing to go, so if you need something else?

BEV. Oh. Yes. One thing. Francine, you remember that big trunk that's upstairs?

RUSS. No no no no. Bev?

BEV. She doesn't mind.

RUSS. Just told you I'm doing it.

BEV. You said it's a two-person job, and here's two of you right here.

RUSS. Well, what's the emergency?

JIM. *(To Bev.)* I *would* offer my services —

BEV. *(Overlapping.)* Oh no no no no no.

JIM. *(Continuous.)* — but I am under doctor's orders, believe it or not.

FRANCINE. Well, I'm just needing to leave by three-thirty.

BEV. *(Resigned.)* All right.

RUSS. Francine? *I* am going to move the gol-darned trunk.

FRANCINE. Yes, sir.

BEV. *(To Jim, mock-private.)* That's what I get for trying. *(Francine exits. Discomfort.)*

JIM. *(To Russ.)* Soooo —

BEV. Did you get any lunch, Jim? Do you want some — ?

JIM. No no no no no.

BEV. Since I guess we're *cleaning out the larder* and Russ seems to be eating every last thing in the icebox, so you'll have to fight him for the ice cream.

JIM. Not for me.

RUSS. *(Shrugs.)* Well, ya know. Can't pack ice cream in a suitcase. *(Bev finds this hilarious.)*

BEV. *(Beside herself.)* In a suitc — *(To Jim.)* Did you hear what he just said?

JIM. *(Chuckling as well.)* Man's got a point!

BEV. *(Slaps Russ's shoulder.)* How do you think of those things? Ice cream in a —

15

JIM. Not unless you're moving to the North Pole! *(Bev laughs harder.)*
BEV. Thank goodness we're not moving *South*!
JIM. *That'd* be a mess. No question. *(Bev and Jim stop laughing, sigh. More discomfort, then.)* No question.
BEV. *(Jumping up.)* Well, I'm going to see what we *do* have. *(Bev exits into the kitchen, leaving Russ and Jim alone.)*
JIM. Whaddya, coming down with something?
RUSS. Who?
JIM. Bev said "under the weather."
RUSS. Me?
JIM. And here ya sit in your PJs —
RUSS. No no no no no. I'm — Took the day to — Truck coming, so —
JIM. I gotcha.
RUSS. Coupla days off.
JIM. Playing hooky.
RUSS. No no.
JIM. Bev's your alibi.
RUSS. Just giving her a hand with stuff.
JIM. And you are hard at work, as I see.
RUSS. *(Smiles a little.)* No. I just.
JIM. Kidding you.
RUSS. I know. I — I — Yup.
JIM. Woulda come to your aid there, only I'm dealing with a little, uh, issue.
RUSS. Oh yeah?
JIM. Piano I told ya about?
RUSS. Right?
JIM. Didja ever … *(Lowers voice.)* ever need a *truss*? Have to wear one of those?
RUSS. Uhhhh…. Don't recall.
JIM. Oh, you'd recall it if you did.
RUSS. Guess not, then.
JIM. Then you are a *fortunate* man.
RUSS. I hear you.
JIM. Bend the knees or suffer the consequences.
RUSS. Yup. *(Brief pause.)*
JIM. So, *Monday*, you said.
RUSS. Yup.
JIM. Off to the hinterlands.

RUSS. Monday it is.

BEV. *(Calling from off.)* Jim, was that a yes or a no on the iced tea?

JIM. *(Calling back to her.)* Uhhh, I would not say no to that.

BEV. *(Same.)* Russ? *(Russ shakes his head.)*

JIM. *(Same.)* I believe Russ is declining your gracious offer.

BEV. *(Same.)* I thought as much.

JIM. *(Back to Russ.) Monday.*

RUSS. Indeed.

JIM. Head 'em up. Move 'em out.

RUSS. Yup.

JIM. And when ya start at that Glen Meadows office?

RUSS. Monday after.

JIM. How about that.

RUSS. Yup.

JIM. And how's that shaping up?

RUSS. Oh, boy, now. That's a nice setup.

JIM. I betcha.

RUSS. And *spacious*, that's the thing. And *carpeted*? And I got a look at that office they're putting me in. Tell you what I thought to myself, I thought what the heck do ya do with all this space? *Corner* office. Windows two sides. But the space is the primary — That is just an … *extravagant* amount of space.

JIM. Elbow room.

RUSS. Other thing is, once we get situated up in the new place. The time it takes? Driveway to the parking lot? Know what that's gonna take me?

JIM. Five minutes.

RUSS. Six and a half.

JIM. Close enough.

RUSS. Timed it. Door to door.

JIM. Roll outta bed and *boom*.

RUSS. And Tom Perricone. I don't know if you know Tom. Colleague of mine. Now, he's going to relocate to that same office and they live right down here offa Larabee. You know what *that's* gonna take him on the expressway?

JIM. That's a drive.

RUSS. Thirty-five minutes. And that's no traffic.

JIM. Well, Judy and I are sure gonna miss having you two around.

RUSS. Well … Yeah. *(Awkward pause.)*

JIM. *(Lowers voice, secretively.)* And how's Bev doing?

RUSS. Oh, you know. Bev loves a project.

JIM. Keep her occupied.

RUSS. The *mind* occupied.

JIM. What, does she worry a lot?

RUSS. No. No more than —

JIM. About you?

RUSS. Me? No.

JIM. Ya seem good to me.

RUSS. I meant — you know how she gets.

JIM. Sure.

RUSS. Overexcited.

JIM. I can see that.

RUSS. Worked up over things. Minor things.

JIM. Things like?

RUSS. Oh, you know.

JIM. Not calling yourself a *minor thing*, are you?

RUSS. *(Beat, slightly irritated.)* No, I didn't — I meant things like —

JIM. *(Chuckles.)* Do *you* consider yourself a *minor thing*?

RUSS. Jim, I didn't — Well, actually, in the grand scheme of things I don't think any one of us is, uh ... particularly — did Bev *ask* you to come over?

JIM. Nope.

RUSS. I mean, good to see you. Great to see you.

JIM. I mean, we *ran into* each other coupla days ago. Got to talking.

RUSS. Uh-huh.

JIM. Little about you. Since she cares about you.

RUSS. Right. Right. *(Russ looks for Bev.)* The heck's she's doing in there?

JIM. Everybody cares about you, Russ.

RUSS. Uh-huh. Uh-huh. Yup. Well. Tell ya what I think. And I'm not a psychiatrist or anything but I do think a lotta people today have this tendency, tendency to *brood* about stuff, which, if you ask me, is, is, is — well, short answer, it's *not productive*. And what *I'd* say to these people, *were* I to have a degree in psychiatry, I think my advice would be maybe, get up offa your rear end and *do* something.

JIM. Huh.

RUSS. Be my solution.

JIM. Uh-huh.

RUSS. Of course, what do I know?

JIM. I think you know plenty. *(Beat. Russ looks toward kitchen.)*

RUSS. *(Calling.)* Hey, Bev?

JIM. Like, I think you know your son was a good man, no matter what. Hero to his country. Nothing changes that.

RUSS. Yup yup yup.

JIM. And I also think you know that sometimes talking about things that happen, painful things, maybe —

RUSS. Uh, you don't happen to have a degree in psychiatry *either*, do you, Jim? *(Jim stares.)* No? Just checking.

JIM. We all suffer, you know. Not like you and Bev, maybe, but —

RUSS. But, see, since what *I'm* doing here is, see, since I'm just minding *my own* business —

JIM. *(Overlapping.)* But it doesn't hurt —

RUSS. *(Continuous.)* — sorta seems to *me* you might save yourself the effort worrying about things you don't need to *concern* yourself with and furthermore —

JIM. *(Overlapping.)* He's in a better place, Russ.

RUSS. *(Continuous.)* — if you *do* keep going on about those things, Jim, well, I hate to have to put it this way, but what I think I might have to do is ... uh, *politely* ask you to uh, *(Clears his throat.)* ... well, to go fuck yourself. *(Pause.)*

JIM. Not sure there's a polite way to ask that. *(Russ rises to exit.)*

RUSS. *(Embarrassed.)* Okay? So.

JIM. I just can't believe Kenneth would've wanted his own father to —

RUSS. *(Maintaining his calm.)* Yup. Yup. So, you can go fuck yourself okay? *(Bev enters with Jim's iced tea.)*

BEV. So wait. So if it's *Napoli* in Italian, then wouldn't adding an "E" before the "A" just seem superfluous — What's happening?

JIM. Bev, I believe I will hit the road.

BEV. What are you — ? Russ?

RUSS. Going upstairs.

BEV. What happened?

JIM. Not to worry.

BEV. *(To Russ.)* What did you do?

JIM. Another time.

BEV. *(To Russ.)* Come back here.

JIM. *(Overlapping, to Bev.)* No no. Russ made his feelings clear —

BEV. *(Overlapping, quietly to Russ.)* Why are you being like this?

JIM. *(Continuous.)* — in no uncertain terms.

RUSS. *(To Bev.)* Going up, now.

JIM. Terms may be more appropriate for the *locker room* than the —

BEV. *(To Jim.)* I *told* you so. I *told* you what it's like. And he uses these ugly words in other people's presence *(To Russ.)* and I'm not some kind of *matron*, but what in the world is wrong with *civility*?

RUSS. Honey? I am not going to stand here with you and Jim and discuss —

BEV. *(Overlapping.)* Well, you're being *ugly*, and I don't like *ugliness*.

RUSS. *(Continuous.)* — *private* matters, matters that are between me and the memory of my son —

BEV. *(To Jim, overlapping.)* I think his *mind* has been affected, I really do.

RUSS. *(Continuous, overlapping.)* — and if the two of you want to talk about Kenneth on your own time, if that gives you some kind of *comfort* —

BEV. And what's wrong with comfort? Are we not *allowed* any comfort anymore?

RUSS. Well, Kenneth didn't get a whole lotta comfort, did he?

BEV. He was *sick*, Russ! And for you to use nasty words to Jim —

JIM. Nothing I haven't heard before.

RUSS. *(Moving upstairs.)* Changing my shirt.

JIM. I was in the service, too, you know.

RUSS. *(Bitter laugh.)* Oh right. And tell me again. How many people did *you* kill?

BEV. *Oh, for god's sake, stop it!!*

RUSS. Sat behind a *desk*, didn'tcha? Goddamn *coward. (The doorbell rings. All stand in silence. Bev covers her mouth. At the front door, we can see Albert peer through a small window.)*

ALBERT. *(From off.)* Hello? *(And still no one moves.)* Anybody home? *(Bev looks to Jim, who opens the door.)*

JIM. Afternoon.

ALBERT. *(To Jim.)* Uh, how d'you do? I'm just here to —

BEV. Francine? Albert's here.

FRANCINE. *(Calling, from off.)* Yes, ma'am. I'm coming.

BEV. She's on her way.

ALBERT. Thank you, ma'am. *(Russ turns and exits up the stairs. Jim does not know whether to invite Albert in or not. He turns to Bev. Bev turns back to Albert.)*

BEV. Albert, would you like to wait inside?

ALBERT. Uh. All right, thank you, ma'am.

BEV. I bet it's warm out there, isn't it?

ALBERT. Ohhh, yes it is.

BEV. Can I offer you some iced tea?

ALBERT. No. Thank you, though.

BEV. Well, I'm sure she'll be right along.

ALBERT. Thank you. *(Albert sits near the door, but within earshot of Jim and Bev.)*

JIM. *(To Bev, whispering because of Albert.)* I think maybe it's time for me —

BEV. *(Rapidly, whispering.)* Oh please don't go, please don't, I just don't want to be alone with him right now. It makes me feel so alone —

JIM. *(Overlapping.)* You're not alone.

BEV. *(Continuous.)* — the way he sits up all night long. Last night he was just sitting there at three in the morning —

JIM. *(Overlapping.)* I know. I do.

BEV. *(Continuous.)* — and I say to him, say, don't you feel sleepy? Do you want to take a Sominex, or play some cards maybe, and he says *I don't see the point of it* as if there has to be some grand justification for every single thing that a person — *(And now she notices Albert rising and heading for the door. To Albert.)* — Wait. Yoo-hoo?

ALBERT. *(Having overheard.)* 'S all right.

BEV. Something wrong?

ALBERT. No no.

BEV. She said she's on her way.

ALBERT. I can wait outside.

BEV. *(Calling off.)* Francine?

FRANCINE. *(From off.)* I'm coming.

BEV. There she is. *(Francine enters in street clothes, with two large bags of hand-me-downs. She stops to put on her earrings.)*

FRANCINE. I'm sorry. I guess I'm moving a little slower than usual.

BEV. And here's Albert waiting so patiently, If only I had *door-to-door service like Francine*!

FRANCINE. So, I'll see you Monday, then.

BEV. Albert, isn't this place just a *catastrophe*?

ALBERT. Oh, yes it is.

BEV. *(To Albert.)* I tell you, I don't know *what* I would do without a friend like Francine here, and on a *Saturday*, I mean she is just a treasure. What on earth are we going to do up there without her?

ALBERT. Well, I trust ya'll can sort things out.

BEV. *(To Francine.)* Oh, and maybe Monday we can see about that big trunk, why don't we?

FRANCINE. We'll make sure and do that.

BEV. I'd do it myself but I'm not a big strapping man like Albert here.

JIM. Afraid I've gotta exempt myself —

BEV. Oh no no no no no. Francine and I can manage.

ALBERT. What's it, a trunk, you said?

FRANCINE. *(With a shake of the head to dissuade Albert.)* A foot-locker.

ALBERT. Where's it at?

BEV. No no no no no we just need to bring it down the stairs.

ALBERT. I don't mind.

BEV. Oh, thank you, but no.

FRANCINE. *(To Bev.)* But definitely Monday.

ALBERT. These stairs, here?

BEV. Oh no no no — I mean, it wouldn't take but two minutes.

FRANCINE. *(To Bev, re: her bags.)* It's just I got these things here to take care of.

ALBERT. I can put them in the car.

JIM. Oh, got yourself a car?

ALBERT. Yes, sir.

JIM. *(Looking out.)* Whatzat, a Pontiac?

ALBERT. Yes, sir.

FRANCINE. *(Significantly, to Albert.)* It's just that I'm afraid we're going to be late.

ALBERT. *(Not getting it.)* Late for what?

FRANCINE. The place we gotta be?

ALBERT. The *place*?

FRANCINE. Remember?

ALBERT. *(To Francine.)* The — What're you — ?

FRANCINE. *(Continuous, to Bev.)* I'm sorry.

ALBERT. *(To Francine.)* Said two minutes is all.

FRANCINE. *(Quiet, pointedly.)* Well, I've got my *hands* full.

ALBERT. I just said I can put them in the —

FRANCINE. *(Testily, as they start to go.)* I can put them in the car. *I* can do that.

BEV. Did you get the chafing dish?

FRANCINE. No ma'am, thank you, though.

ALBERT. *(To Bev and Jim.)* Be right back. *(Albert opens the door to reveal Karl Lindner, about to ring the bell.)*

KARL. *(An oddly formal and uncomfortable-seeming man.)* Ah. Unexpected. Uhhh…?

BEV. Hello, Karl.

KARL. *(Relieved.)* Ah, Bev. Voilà.

ALBERT. *(To Karl, squeezing past.)* Excuse us, if you don't mind?

KARL. Not at all. After *you*, sir. *(Karl makes way for Albert and Francine to pass.)*

ALBERT. *(To Francine, as they exit, barely audible.)* What is the *matter* with you?

KARL. *(From the door, seeing him.)* Ah. Jim, too. Hello, lad.

JIM. Karl.

BEV. *(Unenthusiastically.)* Come on in, Karl.

KARL. Uhhh … *(As if working out a puzzle.)* Yes. *Could* do that. However, you'll recall, Bev, that Betsy currently happens to be, uh, how shall we say — ?

BEV. Ohhh, is it almost that time?

KARL. Uh, point *being*, that she did accompany me.

BEV. What do you — you mean she's in the *car*?

KARL. She is.

BEV. Well, for heaven's *sake*, Karl! Don't leave her out in a hot *car*.

KARL. Well, that was my thinking.

BEV. Bring her *in* with you.

KARL. Will do.

BEV. Of all *things*.

KARL. *(As he goes.)* Back in a flash. *(As Karl exits again, Russ descends the stairs in a clean shirt and shoes. Bev and Jim allow him to silently pass by them. He walks to the chair and collects the ice cream carton.)*

BEV. You changed your shirt. *(Russ continues into the kitchen without responding. As soon as he is gone.)*

JIM. *(Quietly.)* Bev.

BEV. *(Whispering.)* I know I'm being silly. I know I am, but —

JIM. *(Overlapping.)* Not at all. Not in the least.

BEV. *(Continuous whisper.)* — it's just that after two and a half *years* you'd think that with *time*, because that's supposed to be the thing that helps, isn't it? A little bit of time —

JIM. *(Overlapping.)* A great healer.

BEV. *(Continuous whisper.)* — and I thought with the new job and the move I thought somehow he would start to let go of — *(Russ returns from the kitchen. Bev goes silent. He goes to a door beneath the stairs, opens it, pulls a string to turn on a light, and exits. Calling after him.)* Where are you going, the basement?

RUSS. *(From off.)* Yup.

BEV. Are you looking for something?

RUSS. *(Farther.)* Yup. *(The front door opens. Karl escorts his wife, Betsy, who is eight months pregnant, and who also happens to be totally deaf.)*

KARL. Here we are, then.

BEV. Oh, *there she is*!

BETSY. Hehhyoooh, Behhhh. *[Hello, Bev.]*

BEV. *(Over-enunciating for Betsy's benefit.)* Well just *look* at you! My *goodness*. You are just the biggest *thing*.

BETSY. Ah nohhh!! Eee toooor. Ah so beee!!! *[I know!! It's true. I'm so big!!!]*

KARL. Took the liberty of not ringing the bell.

BEV. Betsy, you know Jim.

JIM. Indeed she does.

BETSY. Hah Jeee. *[Hi Jim.]* *(Jim shows off his sign language skills to Betsy, finger-spelling the last word.)*

BEV. Oh, well, now look at *that*. Look at them go. What is that about? Somebody translate!

BETSY. *(Laughing to Karl.)* Huhuhuuh!! *Kaaaaa!!*

JIM. *(Chuckling along.)* Uh-oh! What did I do? Did I misspell? *(Betsy signs to Karl.)*

KARL. *(Chuckles.)* Uh, it seems, Jim, that you, uh, told Betsy that she was expecting a *storm*!!

BEV. *No!* He meant stork! You meant *stork*, didn't you?

BETSY. *(Pantomimes umbrella.)* Ahneemah-umbrayah! *[I need my umbrella!]* *(All laugh.)*

BEV. Her *umbrella*! *(To Betsy.)* I understood that!

KARL. Have to check the weather report!

BEV. A *storm*, I'm going to tell that to Russ.

JIM. Must have rusty fingers!! *(All chuckle.)*

BETSY. *(To Karl, asking for translation.)* Kaaaah?

KARL. *(Speaks as he signs.)* Uh, Jim says *his fingers are rusty. (Betsy laughs and covers her mouth.)*

BEV. See? She understands.

BETSY. *(To Jim, imitating washing hands.)* Jeee, mehbbe yew neeee sooohh!! *[Jim, maybe you need soap!]* *(More polite laughing.)*

BEV. *(Explaining to Jim.)* Soap. For the *rust* on your —

JIM. *(To Bev.)* No, I understood. *(Russ emerges from the basement, carrying a large shovel.)*

KARL. And there's the man himself! Thought he'd absconded!

BEV. *(To Russ.)* The Lindners are here.

BETSY. Hehhyoooo, Ruuuuhhh. *[Hello, Russ.]*

RUSS. Betsy. *(To Bev.)* Ya seen my gloves anywhere?

KARL. *(Re: the shovel.)* Tunneling to China, are we?

RUSS. *(To Bev.)* Pair of work gloves?

BEV. *(To Karl.)* Do you know I just got through saying how Russ and I never entertain and here it is a regular neighborhood social!

KARL. Well, we shan't be long.

BEV. Karl, do you suppose Betsy would like a glass of iced tea?

KARL. *(She does not see him.)* Bets — ? *(To Bev.)* Point to me.

BEV. *(To Betsy, over-enunciated.) Betsy, look at Karl. (Betsy looks at Karl.)*

KARL. *(To Betsy, signing simultaneously.)* Bev wants to know if you want some iced tea to drink?

BETSY. Ohhh, yehhhpeee. Dahhnyoo, Behhh. *[Yes please, thank you, Bev.]*

RUSS. *(To Bev.)* Know the gloves I'm talking about?

BEV. Well, Karl's here. I thought you were going to talk to Karl. *(Francine and Albert have entered and started up the stairs.)*

RUSS. *(Seeing Albert and Francine.)* The heck's going on?

BEV. Nothing. Now, we two girls are going to the refreshment stand, so you boys'll have to manage on your own.

KARL. Have no fear.

BEV. *(While exiting, as before.) So how are you feeling, Betsy? Are you tired?*

BETSY. Noooo, ahhhh fiiieee, Behhhh, reeeee. *[No, I'm fine, Bev, really.] (Betsy and Bev exit to the kitchen.)*

KARL. Now, Russ, Bev tells me you're indisposed, and normally I'd — *(Realizes.)* Ah. Not *contagious*, is it?

RUSS. Is what?

KARL. Hate for Betsy to, uh, come into contact with any —

RUSS. Not contagious.

KARL. Can't be too careful. Or possibly one can. Anyway, hate to commandeer your Saturday afternoon here, *a man's home*, as they say, but, as we haven't seen your face at Rotary of late I thought I might —

RUSS. *(Overlapping.)* What's on your mind, Karl?

KARL. *(Continuous.)* — intrude upon the sanctity of — what'd you say?

RUSS. What's on your mind?

KARL. Ah. Well. Firstly — May I sit?

RUSS. Yeah, yeah.

JIM. Karl, I will be taking my leave.

KARL. Not on my account?

JIM. Parish business.

KARL. Uh, well, truth to tell, Jim, we might actually benefit from your insight, here?

JIM. *(Looks at watch.)* Uhhhhh —

KARL. If it's not pressing?

JIM. Actually —

KARL. Not to usurp your authority, Russ. Your castle. You are the king.

RUSS. What's on your mind?

KARL. *(As he sits on a box.)* Is this safe?

RUSS. Anywhere.

KARL. No breakables? And Jim?

JIM. *(Sits, looking at Russ.)* Uhh … minute or two.

KARL. Good. Good good good. So. *(Bev opens the kitchen door.)*

BEV. Iced tea for you, Karl?

KARL. Ah. Problem *being* that I *do* have some sensitivity to the cold beverages, so my question would be is the tea *chilled*, by which I mean has it been *in* the Frigidaire?

BEV. *(Enduring him.)* No, Karl.

KARL. Then, if I might have a serving *minus* the ice? That would suit me fine.

BEV. All right, Karl. *(Bev closes the door.)*

KARL. Anyway Russ, if you don't mind, I will proceed directly to, dare I say, *the crux*. So. First and foremost, as far as matters of *community* are concerned, I've always maintained — *(Bev and Betsy enter from the kitchen with glasses of iced tea.)*

BEV. All right, you boys.

KARL. *(Panicky about Betsy.)* What's — ? Is something — ?

BEV. *(Handing Karl his tea.)* She's *fine*, Karl.

KARL. Is that tea, she's drinking?

BEV. Yes, Karl.

KARL. Slow sips. Small sips.

BEV. All right, Karl. *(Betsy and Bev sit at the dining table, away from the men. They begin to communicate via pad and pencil.)*

RUSS. You were saying?

KARL. *(Eyeglasses off, mops brow.)* Tad overwrought, I suppose. *(Lowers voice.)* What with Betsy's condition, but … well, given our history of two years ago, I don't know, Russ, if you knew the details of that.

RUSS. Some, yup.

KARL. And Jim: source of great comfort for us during all of that. *(Beat, then to Russ.)* It was the umbilical cord. Nature of the problem.

RUSS. I knew that.

KARL. Wrapped around the … *(Indicates his neck.)* Exactly. So, no one at fault. No one to *blame.* But these tragedies do come along. As you and Bev well know.

JIM. What're you hoping? Boy or girl?

KARL. Ah, no. Touch wood. No tempting fate.

JIM. There you go.

KARL. *(Back to Russ.)* Not to compare *our* little … setback … to what the two of you endured, but —

RUSS. Something about a *crux?*

KARL. Right you are. Well: To backtrack. I take it, Russ, you're aware that the Community Association meets the first Tuesday of each month? And as I'm sure you know, Don Skinner is part of the steering committee. And somehow it came to Don's attention at this late juncture that Ted Driscoll had found a buyer for this house and I have to say it *did* come as something of a shock when Don told us what sort of people they were.

RUSS. What sort of people are they? *(Beat. Karl stares at Russ.)*

KARL. Well. *(Chuckles.)* Uhh … Huh. I suppose I'm forced to consider the possibility that you actually don't *know.*

RUSS. Don't know *what?*

KARL. Well, I mean. That they're colored.

RUSS. Who are?

KARL. The family. It's a colored family. *(Pause.)* So: I contacted the family —

JIM. Wait wait wait.

KARL. *(To Russ.)* You're saying Ted never bothered to tell you?

RUSS. We, uhh … sort of gave Ted free rein on the —

JIM. I don't think you're right on this one, Karl.

KARL. Oh, but I am. Oh, I've spoken with the family.

RUSS. Bev?

JIM. On the *telephone?*

KARL. Oh, no. As a matter of fact, Betsy and I've just come directly from … *(Beat, for effect.)* well, from *Hamilton Park.*

BEV. *(To Russ.)* What is it?

RUSS. C'mere a second.

KARL. Now, Russ: You know as well as I do that this is a progressive community.

BEV. *(To Russ as she joins them.)* What's he talking about?

KARL. If you take the case of Gelman's grocery: That's a fine example of how we've all embraced a different way of thinking —

RUSS. Slow down a second. Bev, get Ted Driscoll on the phone.

BEV. *(To Russ.)* What for?

RUSS. Karl says. Karl is *claiming* —

KARL. Russ, I have met *personally* with the family, and —

BEV. What family?

RUSS. He claims this family. The family to whom Ted sold the house.

KARL. It's a colored family. *(Jim shakes his head.)*

JIM. *(To Karl.)* Sorry, don't we say *Negro*, now?

KARL. *(Irritated.)* I *say* Negro. —

JIM. *(Overlapping.)* Well, it's only common courtesy, and I'm —

KARL. *(Continuous.)* — I say them *interchangeably* —

JIM. *(Overlapping.)* — not trying to tell you how to conduct your business.

KARL. *(Continuous.)* — and of course I said *Negro* to them — No I think we both know what you're doing.

JIM. And furthermore, I don't think Ted would pull a stunt like that.

KARL. Yes. We all admire Ted. But I don't think any of us would accuse him of putting the community's interests ahead of his own.

BEV. Oh, this is ridiculous.

KARL. And I don't think any of us have forgotten what happened with the family that moved onto Kostner Avenue last year. Now, Kostner Avenue is *one* thing, but *Clybourne* Street —

BEV. Waitwaitwait. Karl, are you *sure*?

KARL. I was sitting with them not two hours ago.

BEV. But isn't it possible that they're ... I don't know, *Mediterranean*, or — ?

KARL. Bev, they are *one hundred percent*. And I don't know how much time any of you have spent in Hamilton Park, but Betsy was waiting in the car and I can tell you, there are some *unsavory* characters.

RUSS. Karl?

KARL. But, in the case of Gelman's: I think there was some mistrust at first, having been Kopeckne's Market for such a long time, but in the end of all Murray Gelman found a way to *fit in*.

BEV. And they hired the Wheeler boy.

JIM. Is he the one with the — ? *(Indicates his head.)*

BEV. He's the — you know. *(Does the same.)*

KARL. And *fitting into* a community is really what it all comes down to. *(A very loud THUMP from upstairs.)*

RUSS. The heck is going *on* up there?

KARL. Now, some would say change is inevitable. And I can support that, if it's change for the better. But I'll tell you what I *can't* support, and that's disregarding the needs of the people who *live* in a community.

BEV. But don't they have needs, too?

KARL. Don't who?

BEV. The family.

KARL. Which family?

BEV. The ones who —

KARL. The *purchasers*?

BEV. I mean, in, in, in, in *principle*, don't we *all* deserve to — shouldn't we *all* have the opportunity to, to, to —

KARL. *(Chuckles with amazement, shakes his head.)* Well, *Bev.*

JIM. In *principle*, no question.

KARL. But you can't *live* in a principle, can you? Gotta live in a *house.*

BEV. And so do they.

KARL. Not in *this* house, they don't.

JIM. But here's the real question:

KARL. And what happened to *love thy neighbor*? If we're being so principled.

BEV. They would *become* our neighbors.

KARL. And what about the neighbors you already *have* Bev?

BEV. I care about them, too!

KARL. Well, I'm afraid you can't have it both ways.

RUSS. Okay. Assuming —

BEV. Wait. Why not?

KARL. Well, do the boundaries of the neighborhood extend indefinitely? Who shall we invite next, the *Red Chinese*? *(Albert has tentatively come to the bottom of the stairs, jacket off.)*

JIM. But the key question is this:

BEV. No. Why *not* have it both ways?

KARL. Darling, I came to talk to Russ.

ALBERT. *(From the stairs.)* 'Scuse me, ma'am?

BEV. Why not, if it would *benefit* someone?

JIM. But *would* they benefit?

BEV. If we could make them our *neighbors.*

KARL. But they won't be *your* neighbors, Bev. *You're* the ones moving *away*!

JIM. The question is, and it's one worth asking:

ALBERT. Sorry to bother you?

RUSS. *(Standing to take charge.)* Okay. *(Deep breath.)* Let's *assume* your information is correct. *(Then suddenly, a large green Army footlocker comes sliding down the stairs with a noisy thumpeta-thumpeta-thumpeta-thump. Albert jumps out of the way.)*

ALBERT.	FRANCINE.	BEV.	RUSS.
Sorry, sir, my fault! That was me. That was all my doing.	*(Top of the stairs.) That was my fault! I'm sorry!*	Oh oh oh. What happened? Is everyone all right?	*Aw, for crying out loud!* What the heck is the matter with people *Bev, darn it all!!*

BEV. *(To Russ.)* Why are you shouting? Everything's *fine*, so —

RUSS. *(Overlapping.)* Well, what did I *tell* you?

BEV. *(Continuous.)* — please don't do that, they're just trying to *help*.

RUSS. *(Continuous.)* I *told* you I'd do it. You heard me plain as day.

BETSY. Eeeen *ahhhh* hurrrrhhh daaaaaa! *[Even I heard that!]*

KARL. *(To Russ and Bev.)* Little *mishap*, is it?

ALBERT. Little trouble making the corner, is all.

FRANCINE. *(Now downstairs.)* I'm sorry. It's heavy and I lost my gr —

RUSS. *(To Albert.)* Just leave the darn thing where it is.

BEV.	KARL.	JIM.	ALBERT.
We can't leave it there.	May one be of assistance?	Lend you a hand, if I could, but —	What should we — ? Would you prefer it if I — ?

RUSS. *(To Albert.)* Just, just, just, just *leave* it.

BEV. But it's blocking the way.

FRANCINE. No ma'am, I can step over —

ALBERT. It's all right. I got her. *(Albert helps Francine climb over the box that now blocks the stairs.)*

KARL. Anyway, let's not drag this out *ad infinitum*. *(Russ, fed up, rises and exits to the basement, slamming the door behind him.)*

BEV. *(Overlapping.)* Russ, don't.

JIM. *(To Karl.)* One second, if I might? *(To Francine.)* Sorry. Uh, *Francine*, is it?

FRANCINE. Yes, sir?

JIM. Francine, we've just been having a little conversation here, and I was wondering if maybe you could spare us a couple of minutes of your time?

KARL. What good does that do? Go next door. Talk to the Olsens. Talk to those who stand to lose.

JIM. *(Ignoring him, to Francine.)* I want to pose a little hypothetical to you. What if we said this: Let's imagine you and your husband here, let's say that the two of you had the opportunity to move from your current home into a different neighborhood, and let's say that neighborhood happened to be this one.

FRANCINE. Well, I don't think that we would, financially —

JIM. But for the sake of argument. Say you had the wherewithal. Would this be the sort of neighborhood you'd find an attractive place in which to live? *(Francine hesitates.)*

BEV. Oh, this is so sil —

FRANCINE. It's a very nice neighborhood.

JIM. *(To Francine.)* No, I'm asking, would the two of you — Would your fam — I assume you have children?

FRANCINE. Three children.

JIM. Oh, super. So, with your children, might this be the sort of place, bearing in mind that they, too, would stand to be affected — ?

BEV. This is confusing things! It's confusing the issue!

FRANCINE. *(To Jim.)* It's a *very lovely* neighborh —

JIM. No, be honest. We want you to say.

BEV. *(To Francine.)* I think what Jim is asking, in his way —

ALBERT. He means living next to white folks.

BEV. I — I — I — I — well, yes. *(Pause.)*

FRANCINE. Well —

BEV. Francine and I have, over the years, the *two of us* have shared so many wonderful — *(To Francine.)* Remember that time the *squirrel* came through the window?

FRANCINE. *(Smiling, indulging Bev.)* Yes I do.

BEV. That was just the silliest — the two of us were just *hysterical* weren't we?

KARL. *(Pressing ahead, to Francine.)* Think of it this way.

BEV. *(To the others.)* We still laugh about that.

KARL. I think that you'd agree, I'm assuming, that in the world, there exist certain *differences*. Agreed?

FRANCINE. What sort of differences?

KARL. That people *live* differently.

FRANCINE. *(Unsure.)* … Yes?

KARL. From one another.

FRANCINE. I agree with that.

KARL. Different customs, different — well, different *foods*, even. And those diff — here's a funny — my wife Betsy, now, Betsy's family happens to be Scandinavian, and on holidays they eat a thing known as *lutefisk*. And this is a dish, which I can tell you — *(He chuckles.)* — is *not* to my liking *at all*. It's — *oh* my goodness, let's just say it's *gelatinous*.

BEV. *(Indicating for him to stop.)* Karl?

BETSY. *(To Bev.)* Whaaaaa sehhhhh? *[What did he say?]*

BEV. *(Over-pronouncing for Betsy.)* Lutefisk.

BETSY. Whaaaaaa?

BEV. *Lutefi* — Karl, can you tell her?

KARL. *(Holds up a finger to Betsy.)* In a moment.

BEV. *(Taking up her pad.)* I'll write it down.

KARL. *(To Francine.)* So, certain groups, they tend to eat certain things, am I right?

FRANCINE. I've never had that dish.

KARL. But, for example, if Mrs. Stoller here were to send you to shop at Gelman's. Do you find, when you're standing in the aisles *at* Gelman's, does it generally strike you as the kind of market where you could find the particular foods *your* family enjoys?

FRANCINE. It's a *very* nice store.

JIM. *(Interposing.)* What if we were to say *this*:

FRANCINE. Mr. Gelman's a nice man. *(Bev hands Betsy the pad of paper.)*

KARL. But, I mean, your *preferred* food items, would such things even be *available* at Gelman's?

ALBERT. Do they *carry* collards and pig feet? *(Francine shoots a look at Albert.)* 'Cuz I sho couldn't shop nowhere didn' sell no pig feet. *(Pause. All stare at Albert.)*

JIM. Well, I think Albert's being *humorous* here. *(Karl and Bev laugh, relieved.)*

BETSY. *(Having deciphered Bev's handwriting.)* Ohhhh, *loo-feee*! *[Lutefisk.] (To Bev.)* Ah *lye* loofee! *[I like lutefisk.]*

JIM. But I will say this —

FRANCINE. *(To Karl.)* I like spaghetti and meatballs. *(Karl quiets Betsy.)*

JIM. — You do find differences in modes of *worship*. If you take First Presbyterian. Now, that's a church down in Hamilton Park and I've taken fellowship there and I can tell you, the differences are notable.

BEV. Jim?

JIM. Not a *value* judgment. Apples and oranges. Just as how we have our organ here at Saint Thomas, for accompaniment, whereas at First Presbyterian, they prefer a piano and, occasionally ... *(Chuckles.)* well, *tambourines*.

BEV. What's wrong with tambourines?

JIM. Nothing *wrong*.

BEV. I *like* tambourines.

JIM. I like tambourines as much as the next person. *(Russ returns from the basement. He is calmer.)*

KARL. Well, let me ask this. *(To Bev.)* Excuse me. *(To Francine.)* Francine, was it?

FRANCINE. Yessir.

KARL. Francine, may I ask? Do you *ski*?

FRANCINE. Do I — ?

KARL. Or your husband? Either of you?

FRANCINE. Ski?

KARL. Downhill skiing?

FRANCINE. We don't ski, no.

KARL. And this is my point. The children who attend St. Stanislaus. Once a year we take the middle schoolers up to Indianhead Mountain, and I can tell you, in all the time I've been there, I have not *once* seen a colored family on those slopes. Now, what accounts for that? Certainly not any deficit in ability, so what I have to conclude is that, for some reason, there is just something about the pastime of skiing that doesn't appeal to the Negro community. And feel free to prove me wrong.

RUSS. Karl.

KARL. But you'll have to show me where to find the skiing Negroes!

RUSS. *Karl!*

BEV. Can we all modulate our voices?

RUSS. It's sold, Karl. The house is sold.

KARL. I understand that.

RUSS. The ink is dry.

KARL. And we all understand your reasons and no one holds that against you.

RUSS. Truck's coming on Monday.

KARL. Fully aware.

RUSS. And that's all there is to that.

KARL. *However. (Beat.)* There is *one* possibility.

RUSS. Nope. Nope.

KARL. If you'll hear me out.

RUSS. Don't see the point.

KARL. Because we went ahead and made a counter-offer to these people.

BEV. Who did?

KARL. The Community Association.

BEV. An offer on *this* house?

KARL. Very reasonable offer.

BEV. *(Baffled.)* But, but, but, they just *bought* it, Karl!

KARL. As opposed to the amount for which *you* offered the property, Russ, which was *far* below the assessor's value —

RUSS. *(Overlapping.)* Well, we're entitled to *give* it away if that's our prerogative.

KARL. *(Continuous.)* — for this type of residence, all of which is neither here nor there, since the family *rejected* our offer. However:

BEV. *(To Russ.)* Why are we even *talking* about this?

KARL. Don has pointed out to me, that, as the seller of the property, you do have a sixty-day option to place it in receivership with the transacting bank to indemnify yourself against liability. Now, that's generally with *commercial* properties, but in this instance —

RUSS. *(Slowly, overlapping.)* Nope. Nope. Nope. Nope. Nope.

KARL. *(Continuous.)* — I think that, inasmuch as Ted *deceived* you about the buyers, that the bank *could* still halt the sale and it would be a simple —

RUSS. *(Overlapping.)* Karl?

KARL. *(Continuous.)* — matter of a signature, if I could finish?

RUSS. Prefer it if you didn't.

BETSY. Kaahhhh?

BEV. And for all we know this family could be perfectly lovely.

KARL. Well, that's hardly the point, is it?

BEV. Maybe it's a point to consider.

KARL. Bev, I'm not here to solve society's problems. I'm simply telling you what will happen, and it will happen as follows: First one family will leave, then another, and another, and each time they do, the values of these properties will decline, and once that process begins, once you break that egg, Bev, all the king's horses, et cetera —
BETSY. *(Overlapping.)* Kaahhh?
KARL. *(Continuous.)* — and *some* of us, you see, those who *don't* have the opportunity to simply pick up and move at the drop of a hat, then *those* folks are left holding the bag, and it's a fairly *worthless* bag, at that point.
BEV. I don't like the tone this is taking.
RUSS. *(To Karl.)* Okay. Tell you what.
KARL. And let's imagine if the tables were turned. *(Re: Francine and Albert.)* Suppose a number of *white* families started marching into *their* commun — ? *(To Francine and Albert.)* Well, actually that might be to your *advantage*, but —
RUSS. *Karl.*
KARL. — you do see my point.
RUSS. Need you to stop now.
KARL. Sorry. *(Beat.)* Maybe not handled with the —
RUSS. It's all right.
KARL. — utmost delicacy.
RUSS. But maybe time to let it drop.
KARL. Didn't mean to turn it into a public referendum. *(Beat.)* But you do understand —
RUSS. No no no no no. That's it. You hear me? Done. All done.
(Pause. In the near distance a church bell begins to ring.)
JIM. *(Quietly looking at his watch.)* Is it four o'clock?
KARL. Well, Russ, if I might —
RUSS. Nope. Nope.
KARL. If I could just say this:
RUSS. No. Karl?
KARL. Well, if you'd let me —
RUSS. No. No more.
KARL. Uhhh ... *(Chuckling.)* Bev? I get the impression your husband is telling me I'm not permitted to *speak.*
RUSS. Don't think it's a good idea.
KARL. Well, Russ, I'm going to ask you at least to keep an open — ?
RUSS. *Karl!* What'd I just ask you?
KARL. Well, I think you're being a tad unreasonable.

RUSS. Well, *I* think we've reached the end of this particular discussion.

KARL. Is that right?

RUSS. Afraid it is.

KARL. Just like that.

RUSS. Just like that. *(Another pause.)*

KARL. Then what about this:

RUSS. *Karl?!*

KARL. Well, I believe the Constitution endows me with a *right* to speak.

RUSS. Well, then you can go and do that in your own home. *(Russ crosses and opens the front door for Karl to exit.)*

KARL. Bev...? *(Laughs.)* He's not being serious, is he?

RUSS. Karl?

KARL. *(Laughs.)* Am I being *silenced?*

RUSS. Not going to ask you again.

KARL. Well, this is a new experience for me.

RUSS. So be it.

KARL. Bit like the Soviet Union. *(Laughs.)* I am truly surprised.

RUSS. Well, *surprise.*

KARL. And a little disappointed.

RUSS. Sorry to disappoint you.

KARL. *(Shakes his head.)* A real shame. For all concerned.

RUSS. Well, that's the way things go sometimes.

KARL. Apparently so.

RUSS. Anyway. Appreciate you stopping by.

KARL. I see.

RUSS. Betsy, too.

KARL. Very well.

BETSY. Kaaaaahhhh?

RUSS. Okay then? Okay. *(Silence. Karl stands and looks to Betsy. The two of them slowly exit through the open door, Russ quietly closing it as they go.)*

BETSY. *(Quietly, before the door is closed.)* Kaahhh, whaah happaaahh?

FRANCINE. *(Carefully.)* Miz Stoller, if we're done talking here?

JIM. *(Rising.)* Yes, you know, I think *I* will take this opportunity — *(But Karl abruptly returns, Betsy following.)*

KARL. However:

JIM. *(Quietly.)* Karl, don't.

KARL. *(Very slowly.)* I *don't* imagine that ... this particular family are *entirely* aware of *why* they've found such an agreeable price for the property. Don't suppose they know *that* aspect of it, do they? And let's say someone was to *inform* them of those facts. Let's say *that* was to happen.

RUSS. *(Chuckles dangerously.)* Really don't know when to quit, do ya?

KARL. Because I think that might be an interesting conversation to have.

FRANCINE. *(To Bev.)* So I'll be seeing you on Mon —

RUSS. *(Maintaining control.)* Well, Karl? You go ahead and do what you think is right, but I'll tell you one thing. What you're going to do right now is —

KARL. *(Overlapping.)* Well, I have a responsibility to the community as a whole. I can't afford to —

RUSS. *(Continuous.)* — you're going to take yourself right through that door and out of this house.

KARL. *(Overlapping, continuous.)* — simply pursue my own selfish interests.

RUSS. *(Maintaining calm.)* Man, what a son of a bitch.

BEV. Russ, *don't.*

RUSS. *(To Karl.)* If you honestly think I give a rat's ass about the goddamn —

JIM. *(Overlapping.)* Okay. Okay.

RUSS. *(Continuous.)* — what, ya mean the *community* where every time I go for a haircut, where they all sit and stare like the goddamn grim reaper walked in the barber shop door? *That* community?

KARL. *(Overlapping.)* My wife is two weeks away from giving birth to a *child.*

RUSS. *(Continuous.)* Where, Bev stops at Gelman's for a quart of milk and they look at her like she's got the goddamn plague? That the community I'm supposed to be looking out for?

KARL. A community with *soon-to-be children.*

JIM. The Apostle Matthew —

RUSS. *(To Jim.)* Oh no no no. *I'm* talking now.

BEV. *(To Francine and Albert.)* I am ashamed of every one of us.

BETSY. *(Tugging at Karl's sleeve.)* Kaaaaaah?

KARL. Betsy, wait in the car.

RUSS. Well, you go right ahead and you tell those folks whatever you want, Karl. And while you're at it why don't you tell 'em about everything *the community* did for my son. I mean *Jesus Christ,* Murray Gelman even goes and hires a goddamn *retarded* kid, but *my* boy? Sorry. No work for you, bub.

JIM. People were frightened, Russ.

RUSS. *(Contemptuous.)* Ahh, of *what*? He was gonna *snap*? Gonna go and kill another bunch of people? Send him off to defend the goddamn country, he does like he's *told* only to find out the kinda sons of bitches he's defending?

BEV. *(Forthright.)* He did not do the things they claimed he did. He would never —

RUSS. *Ah, Jesus, of course he did, Bev! He confessed to what he did!* Sit around all day with your head in the sand, it doesn't change the facts of what he *did*.

BEV. Not to innocent people in that country. And not to women or children. I mean, maybe he lost his temper in a —

RUSS. *Ah, for Christ's sake. What do you think happens in a goddamn war?* They told him to *secure the territory*, not go knocking on doors asking *permission*. And if he was man enough to admit what he did, maybe you oughta have the decency to do the same damn thing.

BEV. *(Turning to Francine for support.)* You remember. Francine remembers what he was like. *(Russ makes a sound of disgust and goes to the footlocker. Under the following, he unlocks and opens the lid.)* How he loved to read and think. That's just the kind of boy he was, wasn't it?

FRANCINE. Yes ma'am.

BEV. *(To Francine.)* And the drawings? The most realistic drawings. I think a lot of people didn't realize —

KARL. Bev, it was never my intention to stir up —

BEV. Ohhh, no, I think maybe it was.

KARL. *(Continuous.)* — such acrimonious feelings, but there is a situation, which —

BEV. Well, maybe if you had known my son a little better. If anyone had taken the time, the way that Francine took the time — *(Russ has produced an envelope from the footlocker. He steps forward, removing a letter on yellow legal paper.)*

RUSS. Here you go, Karl. Let's all read a little something, shall we?

BEV. What are you — ?

RUSS. *(Reading.) Dear Mom and Dad.*

BEV. *Stop it!!!*

RUSS. *(Reading.) I know you'll probably blame yourselves —*

BEV. *(Standing, losing it completely.) Russ, stop it stop it stop stop stop it!!!!*

JIM. Russ. Don't.   KARL. *(To Russ.)* I think
                                      you're unstable, Russ. I really do.

BEV. *(Turning back to Jim.)* You see what this is like? You see? *(To Russ.)* Well, I refuse to live this way any longer! *(She goes into the bathroom and slams the door behind her.)*

RUSS. *(Starting over, calmly.)* Dear Mom and Dad.

JIM. Russ?

RUSS. *I know you'll probably blame yourselves for what I've done —*

JIM. Need you tó calm down.

RUSS. And *you* can go fuck yourself.

KARL. Well, *that* is over the line, mister. That is not language I will tolerate in front of my wife.

RUSS. *(Beat, then.)* She's *deaf,* Karl!! Completely — *(Waving to Betsy, fake-jolly.)* Hello, Betsy! Go fuck yourself! *(Betsy smiles, waves back.)* So here's what I'll do for you, Karl: make ya ten copies of this you can hand 'em out at Rotary. Or better yet. Put it in the newsletter. Rotary news: kid comes back from Korea, goes upstairs and wraps an extension cord around his neck. Talk *that* over at the lunch buffet next week.

BETSY. *(Barely audible.)* Kaahhh?

RUSS. And Francine walking in at nine in the morning to find him there. You be my guest, Karl. You go ahead and tell those people what kind of house they're moving into and see if *that* stops 'em, because I'll tell you what, I don't care if a hundred Ubangi tribesmen with a bone through the nose overrun this goddamn place, 'cuz I'm *through with all of you,* ya motherfucking sons of bitches. *Every one* of you. *(All stand in silence. We can hear Bev crying from behind the bathroom door. Russ slowly folds the letter. Finally.)*

JIM. Maybe we should bow our heads for a second.

RUSS. *(Advancing on him.)* Well, maybe I should punch you in the face. *(Russ moves toward Jim, who, in backing away, inadvertently tumbles backward over a box, toppling a floor lamp as he goes.)*

ALBERT.	KARL.	BETSY.	FRANCINE.
Whoa whoa whoa whoa *whoa*!!	Easy now. Easy does it … careful — Betsy, go! Betsy?	Kaahh!! Waaahhhh happneee?!	What in god's name is wrong with alla you people? *(To Albert.)* Stay out of — Don't. Just stay out of —

(Betsy runs out the front door.)

ALBERT. *(Puts his hand on Russ's shoulder.)* Hang on. Let's be civilized, now.

RUSS. *(Whirling on Albert.)* Ohoho, don't you touch *me*.

ALBERT. Whoa whoa whoa.

RUSS. Putting your hands on me? No *sir*. Not in *my* house you don't.

JIM. *(Gritting his teeth as he copes with his hernia.)* I'm all right.

FRANCINE. *(To Albert.)* What the hell d'you think *you're* doing?

ALBERT. Who're you talking to?

FRANCINE. Who do you *think*?

KARL. *(To Russ, as he helps Jim to his feet.)* Very manly, Russ Threatening a *minister*.

ALBERT. *(To Francine.)* Why're you talking to me like th — ?

KARL. *(To Russ.)* Very *masculine. (Karl and Jim exit out the front door.)*

FRANCINE. *(Privately, to Albert.)* I think they're *all* a buncha idiots. And who's the biggest idiot of all to let yourself get dragged into the middle of it? Whatcha gonna be now, the big *peacemaker* come to save the day? *(Karl sticks his head back in.)*

KARL. *(Through the open door.)* You're mentally unstable, Russ!

FRANCINE. *(To Albert.)* Let 'em knock each other's *brains* out, for all *I* care. I'm done working for these people two days from now, and you never worked for 'em at *all*, so what the hell do you care *what* they do? And now I am going to the goddamn *car. (Francine exits. During the marital squabble, Russ has returned the letter to the footlocker and dragged it out through the kitchen. Albert is now left alone in the middle of the room. He stands idly for a moment, then moves to right the overturned floor lamp. As he does, Bev enters from the bathroom, blowing her nose.)*

ALBERT. *(Seeing Bev.)* It's all right. Nothing broken.

BEV. *(Trying to be composed.)* Oh oh oh don't mind that. But thank you so much.

ALBERT. No trouble.

BEV. And do let me offer you some money for your help.

ALBERT. Oh no, ma'am, that's all right.

BEV. Ohhh, are you sure?

ALBERT. Yes, ma'am.

BEV. *(Finding her purse.)* Well, here, then. Let me at least give you fifty cents.

ALBERT. No, now you keep your money.

BEV. Or, how about dollar? Take a dollar. I don't care.

ALBERT. Ma'am?

BEV. Or take two. It's just money.

ALBERT. Happy to help.

BEV. Or take something. You have to take something.

ALBERT. No ma'am. But —

BEV. What about this chafing dish? Did you see this dish?

ALBERT. Well, we got plenty of dish —

BEV. Not one of these. Francine told me.

ALBERT. Well, that's very kind of you, but —

BEV. She said you didn't have one and somebody should take it and —

ALBERT. *(Overlapping.)* But we don't *need* it, ma'am.

BEV. *(Continuous.)* — make use of it, so if you let me just wrap it for you.

ALBERT. *(Finally raising his voice.)* Ma'am, we don't *want* your things. Please. We got our *own* things. *(Pause. Bev is shocked.)*

BEV. *Well.*

ALBERT. *(Gently.)* Trying to *explain* to you.

BEV. Well, if *that's* the attitude, then I just don't know what to say anymore. I really don't. If that's what we're coming to.

ALBERT. Ma'am, everybody's sorry for your loss.

BEV. *(Holding back tears, nobly righteous.)* You know, I would be ... So *proud.* So *honored* to have you and Francine as our neighbors. *And* the two children.

ALBERT. Three children.

BEV. Three chil — We would ... Maybe we should *learn* what the other person eats. Maybe that would be the solution to some of the — If some day we could all sit down together, at one big table and, and, and, and ... *(Trails into a whisper, shakes her head.)*

ALBERT. Evening, ma'am. *(Albert goes. Bev is left alone. After a moment, Russ enters to fetch the shovel. He carries a pair of work gloves. Seeing Bev, he stops, unsure of what to say. Long pause.)*

BEV. Where'd you find the gloves?

RUSS. Under the sink.

BEV. And where are you going to dig the hole?

RUSS. Under the, uh ... What's that big tree called?

BEV. The crape myrtle.

RUSS. Under that.

BEV. Kind of late now, isn't it?

RUSS. *(Shrugs.)* Do it tomorrow. *(He leans the shovel against the wall. He stands idly, apologetically.)* Kinda lost my temper.

BEV. *(Nods, then.)* Well, that's what happens. As we know. *(Russ slowly moves to sit in the chair he sat in at the start of the act, then looks back at Bev.)*

RUSS. Know what I did the other day? Up there at the house?

BEV. What?

RUSS. Driveway to the office. Timed it. Know how long that's gonna take me now?

BEV. Five minutes?

RUSS. Six and a half.

BEV. Well, you'll have a leisurely breakfast.

RUSS. Read the paper. Cup of coffee and *bang*.

BEV. Hmm.

RUSS. Five-oh-seven, right back at your doorstep.

BEV. And what'll I do in between? *(Russ is caught off-guard.)*

RUSS. I, I, uhhh … Well, gee, I guess, whatever you … Any number of …

BEV. Things.

RUSS. Projects.

BEV. Projects.

RUSS. To keep ya occupied.

BEV. I suppose you're right. *(He turns on the radio. Music. He looks back at Bev, who stares into space.)*

RUSS. *(Feebly, with a little sweep of the arm.)* Ulan Bator! *(Bev smiles vaguely. The lights slowly fade.)*

End of Act One

ACT TWO

September 2009. Three o'clock, Saturday afternoon. There is an overall shabbiness to the place that was not the case fifty years earlier. The wooden staircase railing has been replaced with a cheaper metal one. The oak mantelpiece and most of the woodwork have been painted over several times, the fireplace opening is bricked in, linoleum covers large areas of the wooden floor and plaster has crumbled from the lath in places. The kitchen door is now missing, and we can see through to an exterior door. The front door stands propped open.

Lights rise to find six people facing each other in a rough circle. To one side, Steve and Lindsey with Kathy, and to the other, Kevin and Lena with Tom, all dressed in generic casual clothes for a weekend afternoon. It is warm, and some have iced drinks. Lindsey is visibly pregnant. They sit upon improvised seating — crates, abandoned furniture, etc. Steve, Lindsey and Kathy study Xeroxed documents while the others watch. Finally:

TOM. Everybody good?
LINDSEY. I'm good.
STEVE. Good by me.
KATHY. Go for it.
TOM. So, I guess we should start right at the top.
STEVE. Question?
TOM. And I know we all got questions.
STEVE. The terminology?
TOM. So let's go one at a time: Steve.
STEVE. The term *frontage*?
TOM. Right.
STEVE. *Frontage* means?
LINDSEY. Where are we looking?
STEVE. First page.
TOM. *Frontage* means — *(Deferring to Kathy.)* Did you want to — ?

KATHY. *(To Steve.)* Means the portion facing the street.

TOM. Thus, *front.*

STEVE. *(To Tom.)* Portion of the *property?*

KATHY. *(To Steve.)* Of the structure.

STEVE. *(To Tom.)* Or portion of the *structure?*

TOM. The *facade.*

LINDSEY. *(To Steve.)* I'm not seeing it.

KATHY. *(To Lindsey.)* Second paragraph.

TOM. Bottom of the page.

STEVE. Where it says "minimum recess of frontage"?

TOM. Meaning, distance *from.*

KATHY. From the edge of the *property.*

TOM. Exactly.

STEVE. Is what?

TOM. Is the "recess."

STEVE. Not the *frontage.*

TOM. The frontage is what you're measuring *to.*

LINDSEY. Got it.

STEVE. I'm confused.

LINDSEY. And "edge of the property" means as measured from the *curb?*

KATHY. Correct.

TOM. Not from the *sidewalk?*

KATHY. From the curb.

TOM. Uhh — I'll check, but I don't think that's right.

KATHY. Up to and including.

TOM. But the sidewalk falls under the easement.

KATHY. Right?

TOM. So if it's part of the easement then it can't be part of the property, *per se.*

KATHY. *(Shaking her head.)* By definition the property is inclusive of the easement. The easement is legal passage *across* the property.

TOM. I don't think you're right.

KATHY. So, my understanding has always been —

KEVIN. Sorry, but — Does any of that really *matter?*

STEVE. It might.

KEVIN. I mean, I don't see how any of that really —

STEVE. *(Overlapping.)* The language?

KEVIN. *(Continuous.)* — impacts the outcome of the specific problem that —

STEVE. But *I* don't want to get in a situation where we *thought* we found a solution only to have it turn out we're screwed because of the *language.*

TOM. Wait.

LINDSEY. *(To Steve.)* The language is clear to *me.*

TOM. *(Easily.)* And who's being *screwed?*

STEVE. No no no.

TOM. No one's *screwing* any —

STEVE. I didn't mean like *screwed over,* I meant like maybe we *screwed ourselves.*

KEVIN. But how does that address the *height* issue?

TOM. The elevation.

STEVE. *(To Tom.)* But if the elevation is *conditional* on the perimeter, right?

TOM. That's the idea.

STEVE. If I'm reading correctly?

LINDSEY. But the perimeter isn't changing.

STEVE. But we're saying if it *could.*

LINDSEY. But we've established that it can't.

STEVE. But let's say it *did.*

LINDSEY. But I'm saying it won't.

STEVE. But I'm saying *what if?*

LINDSEY. But I'm saying *what did we discuss?* (Kathy's cell phone rings.)

STEVE. *(To Lindsey, with an easy laugh.)* Okay, but do you have to *say* it like that?

LINDSEY. Like what?

STEVE. In that *way?*

LINDSEY. What *way?*

KATHY. *(Looking at her phone.)* It's Hector. I'd better —

STEVE. *(Apologizing to Kevin and Lena for Lindsey.)* Sorry.

LINDSEY. *(To Kevin and Lena.)* Did I say something in a *way?*

LENA. Not that I noticed.

KATHY. *(Answering phone.)* Hi, Hector.

STEVE. *(Explaining to Kevin and Lena.)* The architect.

LINDSEY. Who really oughta be here.

KATHY. *(Phone.)* No, we're doing it now. No, we're here at the house.

KEVIN. *(To Lindsey.)* Well, if you'd rather wait and do this when he *can* be?

STEVE. No no no.

LINDSEY.

(To Steve.) Well, I think we both know what's going to happen. He's going to go completely ballist — I'm just telling you what to expect.	STEVE. *(Overlapping.)* I don't give a — And, I believe he's working for *us*, right? Not the other way around.

KATHY. *(Phone.)* No, we're here with — *(To Tom.)* Tom, I forgot your last name.

TOM. Driscoll.

KATHY. *(Back to phone.)* Driscoll. So, Tom Driscoll and the people from the neighborhood thing. Property-owners … thing.

LINDSEY. *(To Kevin and Lena.)* And can I just say? I am in *love* with this neighborhood.

KEVIN. Great neighborhood.

LINDSEY. *Totally* great.

KATHY. *(Into phone.)* Well, that's what we're trying to prevent.

LINDSEY. And the thing for me is? My current commute? Which is slowly eroding my soul?

KEVIN. How far ya coming from?

LINDSEY. *(Pointedly.)* Glen Meadows?

KEVIN. *(Wincing.)* Ooof.

LINDSEY. Exactly. And if you work downtown?

KEVIN. Where downtown?

LINDSEY. *(Do you know it?)* Donnelly & Faber?

KEVIN. On Jackson, right? Donnelly & — ?

LINDSEY. Yeah, Jackson east of —

KEVIN. Yeah, I'm across the street.

LINDSEY. Where?

KEVIN. You know the big red building?

LINDSEY. I eat lunch in that building.

KEVIN. Capital Equities?

STEVE. You're kidding me.

KEVIN. I kid you not.

LINDSEY. *(To Kevin.)* And from *here* to downtown is like, what, five minutes?

STEVE. *(To Kevin.)* Ya ever meet Kyle Hendrickson?

KEVIN. I *work* with Kyle Hendrickson.

KATHY. *(Phone.)* No, but I do think you're being a *little* paranoid, because we're not going to let that happen.

LINDSEY. *(To Kathy.)* Lemme talk to him.

KATHY. *I'm* not going to let it happen.

LINDSEY. Kathy.

KATHY. Wait. Lindsey wants to —

LINDSEY. Lemme do it. *(Taking phone.)* Hector?

KATHY. *(Rolling her eyes.)* I'm obviously not equipped to deal with —

LINDSEY. *(On phone.)* I thought you were in Seattle.

STEVE. *(To Kathy.)* What's the problem?

KATHY. Tell you later.

LINDSEY. *(Soothing.)* No no no no. Kathy's here. Kathy's not going to let that — *(Lindsey starts to exit.)*

STEVE. *(To the others.)* Spaniards.

LINDSEY. *(Whispering to the others.)* Two seconds. *(Lindsey exits out the front door. Pause. The others wait.)*

KEVIN. *(To Steve.)* Spaniards?

STEVE. Architect, ya know.

KEVIN. Spanish.

STEVE. Temperamental.

KEVIN. Toro toro.

STEVE. Exactly.

TOM. Seemed cool to me.

STEVE. You talked to him?

TOM. On the phone, yeah.

STEVE. He's a good guy. *(Little pause. Then, small talk.)*

KATHY. We were in Spain last year.

KEVIN. 'S that right?

KATHY. Me, my husband. Spain, Morocco.

STEVE. *(Explaining to Kevin.)* I just meant — with all the paperwork and everything? And then we add *him* into the mix?

KEVIN. I hear you.

STEVE. Cooler heads, ya know.

KEVIN. Prevail.

STEVE. Right. *(Little pause. Then, more small talk.)*

KATHY. Spain's fantastic. We did four days in Barcelona. Saw the what's-it-called? The cathedral? Big, crazy — ?

TOM. Sagrada Família.

KATHY. That. Which I loved. Likewise the food. Which I would happily eat every day for the rest of my life.

KEVIN. Paella.

KATHY. Then Morocco. To whatsit. To Marrakech. Which — I don't know how you feel about *heat*? But oh my god. And they keep giving you *hot tea*. Like, how refreshing. And some theory about how you're supposed to *sweat* in order to feel *cool*, which you'll have to explain to me sometime.

TOM. *(To himself.)* Hot in *here*.

LENA. Very hot.

KATHY. *And.* To top it off. I don't want to bore you with the whole ugly saga *but*: when they tell you not to eat the produce? Take heed.

KEVIN. Like Mexico.

KATHY. Because if you ever need to know where to find a doctor at two in the morning in the capital of Morocco when your husband is doubled over with *dysentery* — ?

KEVIN. Whoa.

KATHY. Gimme a call. *(Little pause. All look at door.)*

TOM. *(Re: Lindsey's absence.)* Said two seconds.

KEVIN. *(To Kathy, indicating himself and Lena.)* Went to *Prague* last April.

KATHY. *(To Lena.)* Oh, I *love* Prague. Prague is beautiful.

KEVIN. Very pretty.

KATHY. The architecture?

KEVIN. That bridge?

KATHY. And it's small, is what's nice. So you can do it all in a couple of days.

KEVIN. And then from there to Zurich.

KATHY. Never been to Switzerland. *(With a laugh.)* But I like the cheese!

LENA. *(Formally.)* Can I — ? I'm sorry. I didn't mean to — but I was hoping I could say something to everyone, if you don't mind? *(All stare at Lena.)* As long as we're stopped?

KATHY.	KEVIN.	TOM.
No. Do. By all means.	Go ahead.	Yeah yeah, please.

LENA. All right, well … *(Clears her throat.)* Um, I just feel like it's very important for me to express, before we start getting into the details —

STEVE. Sorry, but — Maybe we should wait for Lindsey? Don't you think? If it's something important? Otherwise —

KEVIN. *(To Lena.)* Do you mind?

STEVE. Wind up repeating yourself.

TOM. *(To Lena.)* That okay with you?

LENA. It's fine with me.

STEVE. But, hold that thought.

LENA. I will. *(Little pause. Tom drums his fingers.)*

STEVE. Meanwhile —

TOM. Meanwhile maybe we should look at page three?

KATHY. Maybe we should.

TOM. Catch her up when she — *(To Steve.)* If that's cool with you guys.

STEVE. 'S cool with me.

TOM. Good.

KEVIN. Let's do it.

TOM. Just 'cuz I gotta be outa here by like four.

STEVE. Forge ahead.

KATHY. Page three.

TOM. Middle of three.

KATHY. Section two.

TOM. Roman numeral two.

STEVE. *(Aside to Kathy, quietly.)* Rabat, by the way.

TOM. *(Beat.)* Whadja say?

STEVE. Nothing.

KATHY. Couldn't hear you.

STEVE. The capital.

TOM. Of what?

STEVE. Morocco. She said Marrakech.

KATHY. It is the capital.

STEVE. No.

TOM. I'd've said Marrakech.

STEVE. Rabat.

KATHY. I don't think you're right.

STEVE. No, it is.

KATHY. But possibly.

STEVE. Definitely. Anyway.

TOM. Anyway —

KATHY. Or, wait. Is it *Tangiers*?

STEVE. Nope.

KATHY. Why am I thinking Tangiers?

STEVE. Dunno.

KATHY. Maybe we just *landed* in Tang — Or wait, no we didn't.

KEVIN. *(To Steve.)* What's the capital?

KATHY. *I* know what it is. Tangiers was the *old* capital.

STEVE. Umm … no?

KATHY. The *historic* capital. *(Lindsey returns.)*

LINDSEY. *So* sorry.

KEVIN. Everything all right?

LINDSEY. *(Returning Kathy's phone.)* It's fine. It's just, he said he was going to be in Seattle so we went ahead and scheduled this without him and now he's feeling a little proprietary — Anyway. Blah blah.

TOM. So, we skipped ahead.

LINDSEY. Great.

TOM. To page three?

KATHY. Middle of three.

TOM. And since I think we'd all basically agree that —

STEVE. *(To Lindsey.)* Hey. *(To Tom.)* Sorry. *(To Lindsey.)* What's the capital of Morocco?

LINDSEY. The what?

STEVE. The capital.

LINDSEY. What are you talking about?

STEVE. Of Morocco.

LINDSEY. Why?

STEVE. Quick. Just —

LINDSEY. I have no idea.

STEVE. Yes you do.

KATHY. *(Explaining to Lindsey.)* I said Marrakech.

STEVE.	LINDSEY.
(To Kathy.) No no.	Marrakech, yeah.
Let her —	

STEVE. No. *Rabat.*

LINDSEY. Whatever.

KEVIN. *(Explaining to Lindsey.)* Trying to figure out what it was.

LINDSEY. Why?

STEVE. She said she went to the capital of Morocco —

LINDSEY. So?

STEVE. — and it's not the capital.

LINDSEY. *(With a shrug.)* Maybe they changed it.

STEVE. Who?

LINDSEY. The Moroccans.

STEVE. To what?

LINDSEY. Whatever it is now.

STEVE. Which is *Rabat*.

LINDSEY. Okay.

TOM. So —

KATHY. Oh, wait. You know what it is? It's *Timbuktu*.

STEVE. … *nnnnnnno?*

KATHY. The old capital. The historic — *(Tapping her temple.)* That's why I — because it was part of our package.

STEVE. Um. Timbuktu is in *Mali*.

KATHY. But the *ancient* capital.

STEVE. Yeah. Of *Mali*.

LINDSEY. I thought Mali was in the Pacific.

STEVE. *(Baffled.)* In — ?

LINDSEY. Where do they have the shadow puppets?

STEVE. *(Sputtering.)* Are you talking about *Bali*?

KATHY. Same difference.

STEVE.

Uhhhh, *no?*	LINDSEY.	
The *difference* —	And who *gives*	LENA.
is that they happen	a shit, any — ?	I'm sorry. I don't
to be *three distinct*	Steve. Steven.	mean to
countries so, I guess	It's whatever you	interrupt any-
I give a shit —	want it to be, okay?	one, but —

(Dan has entered through the kitchen door. Work clothes, mustache, chewing gum. He lingers at a distance.)

STEVE. *(Continuous, lowering his voice, to Lindsey.)* — and could you possibly not talk to me like a *child*?

LENA. *(In the clear.)* Excuse me? *(All turn to Lena.)* I was hoping to say something, if I could?

STEVE. *(Remembering.)* Oh oh oh.

TOM. Right. *(To Lena.)* Sorry. *(To Lindsey.)* Lena had wanted to mention something and it sounded kind of important so —

KEVIN. *(To Lena.)* But you don't gotta ask *permission*.

LENA. I'm trying to be polite.

LINDSEY. We're totally rude.

KEVIN. No, you're not.

LINDSEY. It's my family. Irish Catholic, you know? *Blarney*.

KATHY. *(Raising a hand.)* Please, my husband? Half-Jewish, half-Italian.

KEVIN. Is that right?

KATHY. Get a word in edgewise.

KEVIN. I believe that.

KATHY. Anyway. Lena.

LENA. Thank you.

LINDSEY. Wait. *Lena*, right?

LENA. Lena.

KATHY. Short for Leonora?

LENA. No.

KATHY. I knew a Leonora.

LENA. It was my aunt's name.

LINDSEY. *(Reminding herself.)* Anyway. Lena, Kevin.

KATHY. *(Raising hand.)* Kathy.

LINDSEY. *(Indicating.)* Kathy, Lindsey, Steve —

STEVE. And Tom.

KEVIN. Don't forget Tom.

LINDSEY. Tom we know. So:

DAN. *(From across the room.)* Ding dong? *(All turn to Dan.)*

STEVE. Hey.

DAN. Hey.

STEVE. How's it goin'?

DAN. 'S there a Steve anywhere?

STEVE. Yeah?

DAN. You Steve?

STEVE. Yeah?

DAN. Hector said if there's a problem talk to Steve.

STEVE. That's me.

DAN. *(To the others.)* How ya doing? *(All respond at once.)*

TOM.	KEVIN.	LENA.
Hey. Good.	Doing all right.	Fine, thank you.
STEVE.	KATHY.	LINDSEY.
Personally? Fine.	I'm doing awesome.	Um, I've been better.

DAN. Uhh … Quick question?

STEVE. *(A quiet sidebar.)* Yeah?

DAN. *(Privately.)* So okay. So, we're, uh, digging that trench back there, ya know?

STEVE. Yeah?

DAN. Out in back?

STEVE. Yeah?

DAN. For the conduit line?

STEVE. Yeah?

DAN. Know what I'm talking about?

STEVE. Yeah?

DAN. 'Cuz before you hook up that line you gotta bury that conduit?

STEVE. Yeah?

DAN. And so in order to dig that trench we gotta take out that tree, right?

STEVE. Right?

DAN. Dead tree back there?

STEVE. Yeah?

DAN. 'Cuz those roots, they go down like maybe eight feet?

STEVE. Yeah?

DAN. Which is why we're taking out that tree?

STEVE. Right?

DAN. Didja know that thing is *dead?*

STEVE. *(Rising.)* Hey. Maybe we should — *(To the others.)* Sorry. You guys go ahead and —

DAN. Whoops.

STEVE. *(To Dan.)* No no. It's just — two things at once.

KEVIN. We can wait.

STEVE. No no no. You guys keep — *(To Dan.)* You wanna show me?

DAN. Lemme show ya.

STEVE. Lemme take a look.

DAN. Show ya what we're dealing with. *(Dan and Steve exit out the back door. Overheard to Steve, as they exit.)* Tell ya one thing though, it is *hot* out here. *(Lena fans herself. A little pause, then.)*

LINDSEY. Now I don't remember what we were — ?

TOM. Page three.

LINDSEY. *Right.*

KATHY. Middle of three.

TOM. So. Knowing as we do that the height continues to be the sticking point — and by the way, the reason the petition was drawn up this way in the first place — I mean, nobody wants to be inflexible, but the idea was to set some basic guidelines whereby *if,* say, the height is the problem, like it is here, then one option would be to reduce the total exterior volume, like your husband was saying. And that's the rationale behind the table at the bottom of the page. So what those figures mean, essentially, is that, with each additional foot of elevation beyond the maximum limit, there'd be a corresponding reduction in volume. And the numbers are based on the scale of the *original* structures, which is relatively consistent over the twelve-block radius, and of which this house is a fairly typical example. Now:

KATHY. Except we know they're *not*.

TOM. Not what?

KATHY. Not consistent.

TOM. Saying *relatively*.

KATHY. A lotta variables.

TOM. We know that.

KATHY. *(Beginning a list.)* The size of the lots, for starters?

TOM. Right, but —

KATHY. The year of construction?

TOM. Right, so the hope was that, by establishing a couple of regulations up front, hopefully we avoid this kinda situation in the future, 'cuz, obviously, it's a pain in the ass for everybody. Now, assuming the Landmarks Committee passes this part of the petition next week —

KATHY. *Assuming.*

TOM. Safe assumption.

KATHY. And if the Landmarks Committee really wants to pick that fight with the Zoning Department that is *their* business, but that's a matter of *if and when*.

TOM. *(To Lindsey.)* Why is this confrontational?

KATHY. Because somebody might've raised these issues when the plans went to the Zoning Department five months ago.

LINDSEY. Kathy.

KATHY. I mean, no one had any objection back *then*.

LINDSEY. Can I say? We *talked* about renovation. We discussed it. Because these houses are *so* charming and I know it's a shame — but when you figure in the crack in the sub-floor and the cost of the lead abatement — and in a market like this one? It just made more sense to start from scratch. *(Tom's cell phone rings. He tries to ignore it.)*

TOM. Right. *But*: the Owners Association has a vested interest — Kevin and Lena call me up last month, they say, Tom, we've got this problem, these people are planning to build a house that's a full fifteen feet taller than all the adjacent structures —

LINDSEY. s	KATHY.	LENA.
Nooo … *fifteen*?	It's exactly what the	Fifteen feet,
Is that right?	block is zoned for, Tom.	three inches.

TOM. *(Continuous.)* — and I think we'd *all* agree that there's a mutual benefit to maintaining the integrity — *(Glances at his phone.)* — the *architectural* integrity —

LINDSEY. Wanna get that?

TOM. *(Continuous.)* — of a historically significant — goddamn it — neighborhood. *(Answering.)* Yeah? *(Steve returns, as Tom talks on the phone, leaving the kitchen door open. Into phone.)* Yeah, okay, but don't call *me* with that in the middle of a Satur — ? Well, then give it to Marla. Because it's Marla's *account*. Well, where the fuck is Mar — ? *(To the others.)* Sorry. *(Tom crosses the room to take the call.)*

STEVE. What's happening?

LINDSEY. I don't know.

LENA. You know, it might be a good idea if we all turned off our phones.

LINDSEY. Excellent idea.

KEVIN. *(To Steve.)* Get your problem solved?

STEVE. Did what?

KEVIN. Out back.

STEVE. Yeah, I dunno. They hit something.

LINDSEY. What something?

STEVE. I dunno.

LINDSEY. Something dangerous?

STEVE. I dunno.

LINDSEY. Is it going to *explode?*

STEVE. It's not — *(To Kevin.)* We're putting in a koi pond, and there's a filtration system that has to hook into the municipal — anyway, they ran into some kind of — whatever. So whatzit, page three?

KEVIN. But maybe wait for Tom?

STEVE. *(With a laugh and a shrug.)* ... standing right *there*.

KEVIN. If we're getting into the legal stuff?

LINDSEY. I agree.

KEVIN. 'Cuz, I'm not a lawyer.

STEVE. I'm not a lawyer.

LINDSEY. But, Kathy's a lawyer.

STEVE. *(Re: Tom.)* And he's the one with the time issue.

KEVIN. Long as we're out by four.

STEVE. *(Okay, but.)* It's three-thirty.

KATHY. We'll be done by four.

LINDSEY. *(To Kevin and Lena.)* Sorry about all this.

STEVE. Crazy. *(All turn vaguely to Tom, who gestures apologetically and mouths, "Sorry." Lena sighs, fans herself.)*

KEVIN. *(Small talk.)* When's the baby due?

LINDSEY. Oh. Um, November.

KEVIN. In time for turkey.

LINDSEY. I know.

KEVIN. Boy or girl? *(Steve is about to answer.)*

LINDSEY. No no no. I don't want to know. Ask Steve. Steve saw the ultrasound. *(Fingers in ears, eyes closed.)* La la la la la la la la la la la ... *(Steve mouths the word "boy," then touches Lindsey's knee. Fingers out of ears, eyes open.)* ... la la la — either way as long as it's healthy.

KEVIN. Knock wood.

LINDSEY. But something tells me it's a girl. *(Kevin and Lena nod. Kathy takes out her phone, dials a number, listens. To Lena.)* You guys have kids?

LENA. Three.

LINDSEY. Wow.

LENA. Mmm.

LINDSEY. How great for you.

LENA. Yes.

LINDSEY. Congratulations.

LENA. Thank you. *(Kathy starts to check messages.)*

STEVE. *(Beat, then to Kevin.)* So Kyle Hendrickson?

KEVIN. *(Remembering.)* Kyle Hendrickson.

STEVE. Kyle Hendrickson — *who*, may I add, kicked my ass in the tenth grade?

LINDSEY. *Who* is this?

KEVIN. *(Laughing.)* Wait wait wait. *Little* Kyle Hendrickson — ?

STEVE. Like the *one* solitary black dude in my entire high school.

KEVIN. Kicked *your* ass?

STEVE. *Publicly* kicked.

KEVIN. Kyle Hendrickson's like, what? Like five-*two*?

LINDSEY. Wait. *When?*

STEVE. *(To Kevin.)* Five-five. JV Wrestling team. Tenth grade.

KEVIN. I think that might officially make you — ?

STEVE. A pussy?

KEVIN. Think it might.

LINDSEY. *(To Steve.)* *Who* are you talking about?

STEVE. Okay. Remember I ran into a guy?

LINDSEY. No.

STEVE. Remember last week? I said a guy from middle school?

LINDSEY. No.

STEVE. I was meeting you downtown — oh, and he told me the *joke*?

LINDSEY. Right?

STEVE. The joke I told you?

LINDSEY. I don't remember.

STEVE. The joke about — well, neither do I, at the moment but it was a joke we both thought was funny?

LINDSEY. Okay?

STEVE. Anyway. *That* guy: *That* is Kyle Hendrickson. Who *he* works with.

LINDSEY. *(To Lena.)* Glad we cleared *that* up.

STEVE. Oh oh oh.

LINDSEY. What?

STEVE. Wait.

LINDSEY. What?

STEVE. Wait.

LINDSEY. *What?*

STEVE. The joke. It's about a guy? Remember? Guy who goes to jail?

LINDSEY. No.

STEVE. White-collar criminal goes to jail, remember? And and and they put him in a cell with — ?

LINDSEY. *(Realizing, privately to Steve.)* *Oh* oh oh. No.

STEVE. What?

LINDSEY. Hm-mm.

STEVE. *What?*

LINDSEY. Let's — *(Changing subject, to Lena.)* How old are your kids?

STEVE. *(To Lindsey.)* Whatsamatter?

KEVIN. *(To Lindsey.)* Nine, ten and twelve.

LINDSEY. *Wow.*

STEVE. *(To Lindsey.)* What's your problem?

LINDSEY. Steve.

STEVE. I was telling the joke.

LINDSEY. Later.

STEVE. You said remind me what joke —

LINDSEY. Okay.

STEVE. *(Laughing.)* But now I'm not *allowed* to tell it?

LINDSEY. *(Quietly.)* Stop a second.

STEVE. *(To Kevin.)* Anyway. Two guys stuck in a jail cell —

LINDSEY. *Steven?*

LENA. *(Finally having had enough.)* I'm sorry, and I don't mean to keep interrupting but can somebody please explain to me what it is we're *doing* here? *(Pause. Tom turns. All feel the chill from Lena.)*

TOM. *(Quietly into phone.)* Just send me the fucking document. *(Kathy and Tom discreetly hang up.)*

LENA. I mean, I know I'm not the only person who takes the situation seriously and I don't like having to be this way but I have been sitting here for the last fifteen minutes waiting for a turn to speak — *(All overlap, quietly chastened.)*

TOM.	KEVIN.	LINDSEY.	KATHY.
Hey. Sorry 'bout that.	No one's taking turns.	I'm so sorry. I really am.	Well, Tom was on the phone, I thought.

LENA. *(Continuous.)* — and meanwhile it seems like nothing is even remotely getting accomplished

LINDSEY. I agree. *(A truck horn sounds outside.)*

KEVIN. *(To Lena.)* So go ahead and say what you —

LENA. *(With a tense smile, to Kevin.)* And could you please not tell me when to — ?

KEVIN. I'm not telling —

LENA. *(Continuous.)* They were having a conversation and —

KEVIN. *(Overlapping.)* And now they stopped.

LENA. *(Continuous.)* — I try not to intrude —

KEVIN. Just being friendly.

LENA. *(Continous.)* — on other people's conversations when they're in the middle of them. *(To the others.)* I'm not trying to be unfriendly.

LINDSEY. No, it's us.

KEVIN. No it's not.

LINDSEY. No, it is.

KEVIN. You're being friendly.

LENA. I'm being friendly.

LINDSEY. *(To Kevin, re: Lena.)* She's being friendly.

STEVE. I'm being friendly.

KEVIN. If anybody's not being friendly —

LENA. Well, maybe the *friendly* thing to do would be for us to respect each other's time, would that be all right?

STEVE.	LINDSEY.	KATHY.	TOM.
Yeah. Sure.	*Yes.* Totally.	Was it me? Was it?	Sorry. Really.

LENA. Thank you. *(All murmur quietly.)*

STEVE.	LINDSEY.	KATHY.	TOM.
(To Kevin.) Was I *disrespectful?*	*So* glad some-one has the balls to finally *say* it.	'Cuz seriously, I thought we'd stopped.	No, you guys? Was my fault. That was me.

(Horn sounds again.)

LINDSEY. *(To Lena.)* Anyway.

LENA. Anyway. All right. *(Taking her time.)* Well … I have no way of knowing what sort of connection you have to the neighborhood where *you grew* up? *(Horn again. Steve turns.)*

LINDSEY. *(To Steve, rapid whisper.)* Just shut the door. Just shut the *fucking* —

KATHY.	KEVIN.	TOM.	DAN.
So irritating.	The hell is that?	Did you guys park in the alley?	*(Offstage.)* What??!!

(Steve jumps up and exits to shut the kitchen door.)

LINDSEY. Sorry. *(Continuing Lena's last line.)* The neighborhood where — ?

LENA. And some of our concerns have to do with a particular period in history and the things that people experienced here in this community *during* that period — *(Steve returns to the circle, sits.)*

STEVE. *(Whispering to Lena.)* Sorry.

LENA. — both good and bad, and on a personal level? I just have a lot of *respect* for the people who went through those experiences and still managed to carve out a life for themselves and create a community despite a whole lot of obstacles?

LINDSEY. As well you should.

LENA. Some of which still exist. That's just a part of my *history* and my *parents'* history — and honoring the *connection* to that history — and, *no one*, myself included, likes having to dictate what you can or can't do with your own home, but there's just a lot of *pride*, and a lot of *memories* in these houses, and for some of us, that connection still has *value*, if that makes any sense?

LINDSEY. Total sense.

LENA. For those of us who have remained.

LINDSEY. Absolutely.

LENA. And *respecting* that memory; that has value, too. At least, that's what *I* believe. And that's what I've been wanting to say. *(All nod solemnly for several seconds at Lena's noble speech.)*

STEVE. Um. Can I ask a — ?

LINDSEY.	STEVE.
(To Steve.)	*(To Lena.)*
Let her finish.	Sorry.

LENA. I was finished.

LINDSEY. *(To Lena.)* Sorry.

STEVE. Right. So, um … Huh. *(How to say it?)* So, when you use the word *value*, um — ?

LENA. Historical value.

TOM. You read the petition.

STEVE. Yeah.

TOM. Spelled out pretty clearly.

STEVE. Right. *(To Lena.)* But, what I mean is — So, you don't literally mean … *monetary* value. Right? *(Lena stares.)*

LENA. My great aunt —

STEVE. Or maybe you do.

LENA. — was one of the first people of color to – in a sense, she was a pioneer —

STEVE. No, I understand — and correct me if — but *my* understanding was that the value of these properties had gone *up*.

KATHY. They have.

STEVE. *(To Kevin and Lena.)* Yours included.

KEVIN. That's true.

STEVE. *Way* up.

TOM. And we'd all like to *keep* it that way.

STEVE. But — You're not suggesting, are you, that, when we build *our* house — ? *(Lindsey puts a hand on Steve.)*

LINDSEY. *(To Lena.)* Look, I for one — I am really grateful for what you said, but this is why we sometimes feel defensive, you know? Because we *love* this neighborhood.

STEVE. We do.

LINDSEY. We completely do, and we would never want to to to to carelessly —

STEVE. Run roughshod.

LINDSEY. — over anyone's — And I totally admit, I'm the one who was resistant, especially with the schools and everything, but once I stopped seeing the neighborhood the way it *used* to be, and could see what it is *now*, and its *potential*?

LENA. Used to be what?

LINDSEY. *(Beat.)* What do you mean?

LENA. What it "used to be"?

STEVE. *(Helpfully, to Lena.)* What you said. About the *history* of — ?

LINDSEY. *Historically*. The changing, you know, demographic — ?

STEVE. Although *originally* — *(To Lindsey.)* wasn't it German, predominantly?

KATHY. German and Irish.

STEVE. Depending how far back you —

KATHY. It's funny, though. Even though my *father* was German — but back when *they* were living here —

LINDSEY. Wait, did I know this?

KATHY. I told you that.

LINDSEY. In this neighborhood?

KATHY. *(To Kevin and Lena.)* They went to church at St. Stan's! Isn't that crazy?

KEVIN. Is that right?

KATHY. *(To Kevin and Lena.)* This is the late fifties. *(Laugh.)* My father was a "Rotarian"! But my *mother* — *(To Lindsey.)* She was deaf? I told you that?

LINDSEY. *That* I knew.   KEVIN. Awwww, that's a shame.

KATHY. *(To Kevin.)* Thank you. It was congenital. But then she got pregnant with me and they moved out to Rosemont, anyway, *her* family, they were *Swedish.*

STEVE. *(To Kevin and Lena.)* There was a great article two weeks ago — I don't know if you saw this — about the history of the changing, uh, ethnic —

LINDSEY.	LENA.
Distribution.	Oh, I should read that.

STEVE. — of the neighborhood and how in the seventies, eighties, how that was followed by a period of — of — of — of — of rapid —

KATHY. Decline.

LINDSEY.	STEVE.	KATHY.
No — Not — No —	Of *growth.*	I don't mean
	Of *growing.*	*decline* —

KATHY. — I mean there was *trouble.*

LINDSEY. Not *trouble*, she didn't mean —

KEVIN. There was trouble.

LINDSEY. *Economic* trouble.

KEVIN. Drugs are trouble.

KATHY. That's what I'm saying.

KEVIN. Violence is trouble.

KATHY. *(Vindicated.)* Exactly.

LINDSEY. And the violence as an *outgrowth* of the criminalization of those drugs.

KEVIN. *(Re: himself and Lena.)* 'Cuz ya know, the two of us wuz both crackheads. *(A frozen moment, then.)*

STEVE.	LINDSEY.	KATHY.	KEVIN.
That's funny. I know you're kidding but that *was* the perception at the — *(To Lindsey.)* — he's *being funny.*	No, come on. Don't say that. Really. Even as a joke.	I know you're joking, but that is exactly what people *thought.*	*(Laughs.)* I'm kidding you. I'm just messing with you.

LINDSEY. I know he was, and it *was* funny but when people are systematically *dehumanized* — If you've been placed in some faceless, institutional —

KATHY. *(Explaining to Kevin and Lena.)* The projects.

LINDSEY. — I mean, like it or not, that kind of environment is not conducive to — to — to — to —

KEVIN. That's true.

LINDSEY. — the formation of *community.*

KATHY. Horrible.

KEVIN. Tough place to grow up.

LINDSEY. With the effect on *children?*

KEVIN. On anyone.

LINDSEY. And to take what had been a pros — well, not prosperous, but a solidly middle-class, um — ?

STEVE. Enclave.

LINDSEY. And then *undermine* the entire economic —

STEVE. Infrastructure.

LINDSEY. — by *warehousing* people inside of these —

STEVE. But that's the thing, right? If you construct some artificial *semblance* of a community, and then isolate people *within* that — I mean, what would be the definition of a *ghetto,* you know? A *ghetto* is a place, where —

LINDSEY. *(Overlapping, to Steve.)* But who *uses* that word? I don't.

STEVE. *(Continuous.)* — where, where, where people are *sequestered,* right? *(To Lindsey, defensively.)* The *definition,* I'm saying.

LENA. Well, *my* family —

STEVE. Like Prague. If you think of — *(Pedagogically.)* Okay: Prague had this ghetto, right? A Jewish ghetto?

LENA. *(Thanks for the lecture.)* We've been to Prague.

LINDSEY. Ohmigod. Prague is *beautiful. (Kevin wiggles his hand.)* I loved Pr — you didn't love it?

KEVIN. Prague's *crowded.*

KATHY. And the food sucks. Or is that just me?

STEVE. But I'm saying, it's not like, one day all these Jews were sitting around Prague, looking at the real-estate section, going, *"Hey here's an idea! Let's all go live in that ghetto!"* Right? *(A beat where they all avoid Steve's comment. Then.)*

LINDSEY. *(To Lena.)* When were you in Prague?

LENA. Last April.

KEVIN. First Prague, then Zurich.

LINDSEY. I want to go back.

KEVIN. *(To Steve.)* D'you ski? *(A laugh erupts from Lindsey.)*

LINDSEY. *(Re: Steve.) Him?*

STEVE. You mean — like *downhill?*

LINDSEY. *That* I'd like to see.

KEVIN. Ever been to Switzerland?

STEVE. *(To Lindsey, defensive.)* I can *ski.* I *have* skied.

LINDSEY. Get that on video.

STEVE. Why is that funny?

LINDSEY. *(Trying not to laugh, to Kevin.)* Sorry.

STEVE. Seriously. What is it about the idea of me skiing that you find so highly, uh — ?

LINDSEY. Anyway.

STEVE. — *risible?*

KEVIN. *(To Steve.)* I just meant, you like to golf, you go to *Scotland.* And if you like to *ski?*

LINDSEY. *(Still laughing.)* Just trying to picture it.

STEVE. Gratuitous.

TOM. *(Refocusing the others.)* Annnnnnyway.

LENA.	LINDSEY.	KATHY.
Yes. Maybe we should try to stick to the topic at hand.	Okay. Tom's right. Let's get it together.	*(To Kevin.)* I can't ski because I was born with weak ankles. Anyway.

LINDSEY. *(To Tom.) Where* were we?

TOM. Page three.

LINDSEY. Uggh. You're kidding.

TOM. Nope.

LINDSEY. How can we still be — ?

TOM. I dunno.

LINDSEY. How is that possible?

TOM. *(Glancing at watch.)* And it is now … quarter to four.

LENA. I'm sorry for taking time.

LINDSEY. No. What you said was *great*.

LENA. And I wasn't trying to *romanticize*.

LINDSEY. You didn't.

LENA. Nothing *romantic* about being poor.

LINDSEY. But, it was your *neighborhood*.

KATHY. *(To Lena.)* Wait, what street?

LENA. Offa Larrabee.

KATHY. My parents lived on Claremont!!

KEVIN. Ya'll would've been neighbors.

LENA. But I didn't mean to make it about my personal *connection* to the house. It's more about the *principle*.

KEVIN. But you can't *live* in a *principle*.

LINDSEY. You had a personal connection?

KEVIN. To the house.

LINDSEY. To *this* house?

KEVIN. *(To Lindsey.)* Her aunt.

LENA. I don't want to — let's not.

KEVIN. Lived here.

STEVE. Wait. *Who?*

LENA. Sort of beside the point, but yes.

KEVIN. *Great* aunt

LENA. On my mother's side.

LINDSEY. You don't mean, *here*, here?

LENA. And this is fifty years ago.

LINDSEY. Here in this *house*.

LENA. For quite some time, actually.

LINDSEY.   STEVE.
(Hand to her heart.) Oh my g — !   *Whoa.*
So so so wait, so — ?

STEVE. *(Clarifying.)* This *exact* house.

LINDSEY. *(How weird.)* — so, like, you've … *been in this room?*

LENA. I used to climb a tree in the backyard.

LINDSEY. Oh my god.   STEVE. Whoa.

LENA. A crape myrtle tree?

KATHY. Well, that is just bizarre.

KEVIN. Any rate, her great aunt — and she had to save a long time to be able to afford a house like this.

LENA. She was a domestic worker. *(Kathy, Lindsey and Steve make sympathetic faces.)*

LINDSEY.	KATHY.	STEVE.
Ohh. Wow.	Tsk. Ohhhhh.	Okay.

KEVIN. And, a house isn't cheap.

LENA. Not *here*, anyway.

KEVIN. Here at *that* time.

LENA. At *that* time — well, when *I* was growing up I really don't remember seeing a single white face in the neighborhood for pretty much my entire —

KEVIN. Well, one, you said.

LENA. Who?

KEVIN. What's his name?

LENA. Mr. Wheeler?

KEVIN. Mr. Wheeler.

LENA. *(To the others.)* I don't think anybody knew his first name.

KEVIN. He was a … what?

LENA. *(To Lindsey.)* At the grocery store.

KEVIN. Bagged the groceries.

LENA. At the Sup'r — Well, back then it was Gelman's but they tore down Gelman's.

KEVIN. And that became Sup'r Sav'r?

LENA. Well, then they tore down Sup'r Sav'r, so —

KEVIN. You know where the Whole Foods is?

STEVE. And what happened to Mr. Wheeler?

KEVIN. Dead, probably.

LENA. He was, you know … *(Touches her head.)* developmentally…?

LINDSEY.	STEVE.	KATHY.
Ohhhh. That's so sad.	Huh. Wow. Depressing.	Ohhhh … you know why that upsets me? I have a niece with Asperger's syndrome.

LENA. But, given the makeup of the neighborhood at that time and the price of a home like this one, the question naturally arises as to whether it was the thing that happened here in the house — whether that in some way —

KEVIN. Played a factor.

LENA. In making a place like this affordable. For a person of her income. *(All stare.)*

STEVE. The *thing*.

LENA. The sad — you know.

LINDSEY. I don't.

LENA. The tragic —

KEVIN. Thing that happened.

LINDSEY. What thing?

KEVIN. *(No big deal.)* Well. Long time ago, but —

STEVE. In *this* house?

LENA. I'm just saying that, since she was one of the very first people of color —

LINDSEY. Wait. Something happened in the house?

STEVE. What, somebody *died*, or — ?

KEVIN. 'S not important.

LINDSEY. That we should be concerned about?

KEVIN. No no no no no.

LENA. Just that — there'd *been* a family. Who had a son who'd been in the Army.

KEVIN. Korea, maybe?

LENA. And who, well, a few years after he came back from the war —

KEVIN. Killed himself.

LINDSEY. *(Beat.)* Oh my god.

KEVIN. Yeah.

STEVE. Wow.

LINDSEY. *Oh* my god.

KEVIN. Sad.

STEVE. Wow.

LINDSEY. Oh my god.

LENA. Which my great aunt didn't know at the time.

LINDSEY. Oh my god, that is just —

LENA. Though I assumed you *did*.

STEVE. Umm, no?

LINDSEY. That is just — just — just — Wait. And they went ahead and *sold* the house to — ?

LENA. Mm-hmm.

STEVE. Wow.

LINDSEY. Without *telling* her that? Because nobody ever told *us* that.

KATHY. Well, they *wouldn't*, would they?

KEVIN. *(Dismissive.)* Fifty *years* ago.

LINDSEY. *(To Kathy.)* But *legally*, I mean, don't you have to *tell* people that?

KATHY. Not if you want to sell it.

LENA. It was something like he'd come back from the Army. And he'd been accused of something.

66

KEVIN. Killing people.

LENA. Innocent people.

KEVIN. Killing civilians.

LENA. And then — you know. Himself.

STEVE. But you don't mean, like like like like … *(Laughs.)* like *here* in this very — ?

LENA. No — I mean, not *where we're sitting.*

KEVIN. Upstairs, wasn't it?

LINDSEY. *(Freaking out.)* I — I — I — I —

STEVE. *(Touching Lindsey.)* Breathe.

LINDSEY. *(Pushing Steve's hand away.)* Stop it.

LENA. I mean, the version *I* was told was, that he went upstairs.

KEVIN. Hanged himself.

LINDSEY. *(Standing, walking away.)* Okay. *No.* No, I'm sorry, but that is *wrong.*

STEVE. *(Following her.)* Where are you going?

LINDSEY. That is just — *No.* To sell someone a —a — a *house,* where — ?

STEVE. Whatsamatter? *(Steve and Lindsey exit to the kitchen, from where we clearly hear:)*

LINDSEY. *No.* There should be a *law.* And I don't care *how,* okay? I don't want to know *how* he did it or in *what room* — Because I'm sorry, but that is just something that, from a legal standpoint, you should have to *tell* people!

KATHY. *(Calling to Lindsey.)* It's not.

LINDSEY. *(From off.)* Well, it *fucking* well should be.

STEVE. Hey. Hey.

LINDSEY. *(Lindsey returns to the room, Steve following.)* And now I have this horrifying *image* in my head?

STEVE. *(To Lindsey, laughing.)* But why d'you have to make such a big *deal* outta — ?

LINDSEY. Uh, it *is* a big deal, Steve. If your *child* — if *our family* is going to *live* in a house where — ?

STEVE. *(Laughing, to the others.)* I mean, it's not like he's still *hanging* up there!

LINDSEY. *(Losing her shit, to Steve.)* It's not *funny,* okay?!! *It's not funny to me, so why are you acting like an asshole?!! (The kitchen door bangs open and Dan noisily enters.)*

DAN. *(Calling out.)* Okay. Show ya whatcha got. *(He drags a large trunk — the same trunk we saw in Act One, covered with mold and dirt — into the middle of the room.)* So that's your problem right there. *(Coughs a couple of times.)* 'Scuse me. And I tell ya one thing: yank this up from down there, take a look at it, you know the first thing I'm thinking to myself? You know what I'm thinking? *Buried treasure.* Like Spanish doubloons or something and I know you're thinking Dan ya crazy bastard but I tell ya what. I know a guy. *(He joins the circle. Coughs again.)* 'Scuse me. This guy. Last summer he's taking out a septic system — this house out in Mundelein. He's sitting on top of his backhoe. All of a sudden *clang.* And this guy's not exactly the sharpest tool in the box, if ya know what I mean, but he goes down in there about five, six feet with a chain and a winch — swear to god – ya know what he pulls out from down there? He stands back. He takes a look — *(Without stopping.)* — You're in the middle of something.

STEVE. Sorta.

DAN. My bad.

STEVE. No no.

DAN. Bull in a china shop.

STEVE. It's cool.

DAN. According to my wife.

STEVE. Oh yeah?

DAN. As well as a couple other names not suitable for mixed — Anyways.

STEVE. Thanks

DAN. *(Re: the trunk.)* I'll just leave this here for ya.

STEVE. Thank you.

DAN. Need me to open it, you lemme know.

STEVE. Great.

DAN. Problem, though. *(Indicating the large padlock.)* Problem's this puppy right here. Now the deal is: I got a saw. Take a hacksaw you could maybe saw it off but whatcha really want is a pair of bolt cutters and I don't think I got any bolt cutters, so.

STEVE. Ah, well.

DAN. 'Cuz you never know. Turns out to be fulla Spanish doubloons we'll haveta split it six ways, huh?

LINDSEY. *(To Dan, taking over.)* Sorry.

DAN. Whoops.

LINDSEY. I don't know your name.

DAN. *(Extending hand.)* Dan.

LINDSEY. Hi Dan.

DAN. Dan or Danny.

LINDSEY. Great.

DAN. *Daniel* when the wife gets pissed.

LINDSEY. But listen —

DAN. No no no no no no I gotcha.

LINDSEY. If you wouldn't mind?

DAN. Middle of your thing and I come barging right into —

LINDSEY. Thank you.

DAN. But you findya some bolt cutters you'll be in business.

LINDSEY. We will.

DAN. *(An idea.)* Hey, ya know what? Hang on a second. *(Dan heads to the back door. As he does:)*

TOM. So I'm just going to push ahead, if that's okay?

DAN. *(Calling out the door, top of his lungs.)* Ramirez!!!

TOM. 'Cuz we still got seventeen pages to cover —

LINDSEY. *(To all.)* And I'm sorry I lost my shit. No, I did. But I think we're both wound a little tight right now with the baby and the house and the money and everything —

DAN. *Ramirez!!*

LINDSEY. — and then to top it all off, we get sent this petition in the mail, you know, and suddenly our entire lives are thrown into chaos at the very same moment that — I mean, the demolition was scheduled to start on Monday and unless we get this resolved which I want as much as anyone then what do people expect?

DAN. *Ram* — *!!!* Ah, screw it. *(Dan gives up, exits.)*

TOM. *(Continuing.)* So: couple of options. One, as we said, is reducing the height —

KATHY. *(Adamantly.)* No. Tom, I'm sorry, but you can't just call an architect at the eleventh hour and snap your fingers and say can you completely redesign an entire —

LINDSEY. It's a little late in the day for that.

LENA. I'm sorry you're upset.

LINDSEY. I'm not upset. I'm not.

KATHY. And may I remind everybody that these guys are under no obligation, legal *or* otherwise —

TOM. *(From a document.)* Okay. Here's the wording from the city council, and I quote: "In recognition of the *historic* status of the Clybourne Park neighborhood, and its distinctive collection of *low-rise single-family homes* —

KEVIN.	LINDSEY.	TOM.
Hey. Hey.	Aren't *we* a	*(Continuous.)* " — *intended*
Everything's cool.	single family?	*to house a community of*
		working-class families. "

LINDSEY. And you know, the thing is? Communities change.

STEVE. They do.

LINDSEY. That's just the reality.

STEVE. It is.

LENA. And some change is inevitable, and we all support that, but it might be worth asking yourself who exactly is *responsible* for that change? *(Little pause.)*

LINDSEY.	KEVIN.
I'm not sure what you — ?	Wait, what are you trying to — ?

LENA. I'm asking you to think about the motivation behind the long-range political initiative to change the face of this neighborhood. *(Another little pause.)*

LINDSEY.	STEVE.	KEVIN.
What does that mean? *(To*	*(To Lena.)* Wait,	The long-range
Steve.) Do you know what	say that again?	*what*?
that means?		

LENA. I mean that this is a highly desirable area.

STEVE. Well, *we* desire it.

LENA. I know you do.

LINDSEY. Same as you.

LENA. And now the area is *changing*.

KATHY. And for the *better*, right?

LENA. And I'm saying that there are certain economic interests that are being served by those changes and others that are not. That's all.

STEVE. *(Suspiciously.)* And ... *which* interests are being — ?

LENA. *(Systematically.)* If you have a residential area, in direct proximity to *downtown*?

STEVE. Right?

LENA. And if that area is occupied by a particular *group*?

STEVE. Which group? LINDSEY. *(To Lena.)* You know what? We're talking about *one house*.

LENA. *(To Lindsey.)* I understand that.

STEVE. Which group?

LINDSEY. A house for our *family*?

STEVE. Which group?

LENA. That's how it happens.

LINDSEY. In which to raise our *child*?

STEVE. No no. Which group.

LENA. It happens one house at a time.

STEVE. Whoa. Whoa. Whoa. Okay. Stop right there.

LINDSEY. What are you doing?

STEVE. No. I'm sorry, but can we just come out and *say* what it is we're actually — ? Shouldn't we maybe *do* that? Because if *that's* what this is really about, then … Jesus, maybe we oughta save ourselves some time and and and and just … *say* what it is we're really *saying* instead of doing this elaborate little *dance* around it. *(Dead stop. All stare at Steve.)* Never mind.

KATHY. *What* dance?

STEVE. I — I — I — I shouldn't have — whatever.

LENA. *(Parsing his meaning.)* So … you think I haven't been *saying* what I *actually* — ?

STEVE. *(Laughs.)* Uhhh … Not to my way of thinking, no.

LENA. Well, what is it you *think* I'm — ?

STEVE. I — I — I … *(Laughs incredulously.)* … like we don't all *know*?

LINDSEY. *I* don't.

STEVE. Oh, *yes you do*. Of *course* you do.

KEVIN. Well, maybe you oughta *tell* us what *you* think she was saying.

STEVE. Oh oh, but it has to be *me*?

LENA. Well, you're the one who raised the question as to —

STEVE. *(Laughs, overlapping.)* Oh, *come on*. It was *blatant*.

LENA. *(Continuous.)* — the sincerity of my speech.

LINDSEY. What the fuck, Steve?

STEVE. You know what? Forget I said it.

LINDSEY.	LENA.	STEVE.
You didn't *say* anything.	Oh no, I'm *interested*.	Let's forget the whole —

STEVE. *(Continuous.)* — Okay. Okay. If you really want to — It's … *(Tries to laugh, then, sotto voce.)* … it's *race*. Isn't it? You're trying to tell me that that … That implicit in what you *said* — That this entire conversation … isn't at least *partly* informed — *am I right*? *(Laughs nervously.)* By the issue of … *(Sotto voce.)* of *racism*? *(Beat, then.)*

LINDSEY.	STEVE.
(To Steve.) Are you out of your — ? I have no idea where this is coming from.	*(To Lindsey.)* And *please* don't do that to me, okay? I've asked you repeatedly.

LENA. Well, the *original* issue was the inappropriately large *house* that —

STEVE. *(Overlapping.)* Oh, come *on.*

LENA. *(Continuous.)* — you're planning to build. Only, *now* I'm fairly certain that I've been called a *racist.*

STEVE. But I didn't say that, did I?

LENA. *Sounded* like you did.

STEVE. *(To Kevin.)* Did I say that?

KEVIN. Yeah, you kinda did.

STEVE. In what way did I say that?

KEVIN. Uh, *somebody* said racism.

STEVE. — *Cism!* — *Cism!* Not — *cist!!*

KEVIN. Which must originate from *somewhere.*

STEVE. And which we all find totally reprehensi —

KEVIN. So — are *you* the racist?

STEVE. Can I just — ?

KEVIN. Is it your wife?

KATHY. Don't look at *me.*

STEVE. Look:

KEVIN. 'Cuz, by process of elimination —

STEVE. Here's what I'm saying:

LINDSEY. What *are* you saying?!

STEVE. I'm saying: Was race not a factor —

LINDSEY. *(Re: Steve, exonerating herself.)* I don't know this person.

STEVE. Were there *not* these differences —

LINDSEY. *What* differences?!! There's no —

STEVE. *(To Lindsey re: Lena.)* Okay: She walks in here, from the very beginning, with all these *issues* —

LENA. *(Overlapping.)* About your *house.*

STEVE. *(Continuous.)* — and I'm only asking whether, were we not, shall we say — ?

LINDSEY. You're *creating* an issue. *Where none exists.*

STEVE. Oh oh oh you *heard* what she *said.* She as much as claimed that there's some kind of, of, of *secret conspiracy* —

LENA. Oh, it's not a *secret.*

KEVIN.	LENA.	STEVE.
(To Lena.) Ohh, *c'mon.* Are you *seriously* — ?	*(To Kevin.)* Oh please, don't be purposely *naïve.*	*There. Thank you. Now you see what I'm* — ?

LENA. This has been under discussion for at least *four decades* now, at the highest institutional levels of —

KEVIN. *(Overlapping, to Lena.) You can't prove that.*
LENA. *(Continuous, with Kevin.)* — oh, don't act like you don't know it's true.
STEVE. *(To Lena.)* What, and now we're the evil invaders who are —
LINDSEY. *(To Steve.) She never said that!!!!*
STEVE. — appropriating your *ancestral homeland?*
LINDSEY. *(To Steve.)* This, this, this — No. I'm sorry, this is the most *asinine* — *(To Lena and Kevin.)* Half of my friends are black!
STEVE. *(Sputtering.)* What??!!
LINDSEY. *(To Steve, as to a child.)* As is true for most *normal* people.
STEVE. Name *one.*
LINDSEY. *Normal* people? Tend to have *many* friends of a diverse and wide-ranging —
STEVE. You can't name *one!*
LINDSEY. Candace.
STEVE. *(Beat, then.)* Name another.
LINDSEY. *I don't have to stand here compiling a list of —*
STEVE. You said *half.* You *specifically* —
LINDSEY. Theresa.
STEVE. *She works in your office!! She's not your "friend."*
LINDSEY. *She was at the baby shower, Steve! I hope she's not my enemy!!*
TOM. Well, this is all fascinating —
STEVE. *(To Lindsey.)* Name another.
TOM. And while I'd love to sit here and review *all* of American history *maybe* we should concentrate on the plans for your *property* —
STEVE. *(Overlapping.)* Yes!! Yes!!
TOM. *(Continuous.)* — which *had* been the *original* topic of the convers —
STEVE. *(Overlapping, continuous.)* The history of America *is* the history of private property.
LENA. That may be —
STEVE. Read de Tocqueville.
LENA. — though I rather doubt *your* grandparents were *sold as* private property.
STEVE. *(To Kevin and Lena.)* Ohhhhh my *god.* Look. Look. Humans are *territorial*, okay?
LINDSEY. *(To Steve.)* Who *are* you?
STEVE. This is why we have *wars.* One group, one *tribe*, tries to usurp some *territory* — and now *you guys* have *this* territory, right? And you don't like having it *stolen away* from you, the way white

73

people stole everything else from black America. *We get it,* okay? And we *apologize.* But what *good* does it do, if we perpetually fall into the same, predictable little euphemistic tap dance around the topic?

KEVIN. You know how to tap dance?

STEVE. *See? See what he's doing?!!*

LINDSEY. Maybe quit while you're ahead.

STEVE. No. I'm sick of — *No.* Every *single word* we say is — is — is *scrutinized* for some kind of latent — Meanwhile you guys run around saying n-word this and n-word that and *whatever.* We all know *why* there's a double standard but I can't even so much as repeat a fucking *joke* that *the one black guy I know told me* —

KEVIN. *So tell the goddamn joke.*

STEVE. Not *now!!*

KEVIN. If you feel so *oppressed,* either go ahead and *tell it* —

LINDSEY. *(To Steve.)* Do *not.*

KEVIN. — or maybe you could *move on.*

LINDSEY. *(With finality.) Thank you!*

LENA. Well, I want to hear it.

KEVIN.	LENA.	LINDSEY.
(To Lena.) Ohh, *don't* —	*(To Kevin.)* Why not? You're not interested?	No. Trust me. It's offensive.

STEVE. *(To Lindsey.)* Of course it's *offensive* —

LINDSEY. *(Overlapping.)* To *me.* Offensive to *me.*

STEVE. *(Continuous.)* — that's the whole point of the — How? How does it offend *you?*

LINDSEY. Because it's disgusting and juvenile and traffics in the worst possible type of obsolete bullshit stereotypes.

LENA. *(Beat, then.)* Well, now I *gotta* hear it.

KEVIN.	STEVE.	LINDSEY.
No no no no no. Aww, *c'mon.*	No. I can't.	Not while I'm in the room.

LENA. *(To Kevin, re: Lindsey.)* Well, she says it's so offensive, and I have no way of knowing if she's right, and if I don't ever *hear* it, how will I ever *know?* *(Kevin sighs, throws up his hands.)*

STEVE. Um, you know what? I don't even remember it now.

LENA. Two men in jail, you said.

KATHY. Oh, *I* know this one.

LINDSEY. *(A warning.) Steven?*

LENA. Wasn't that it? Two men...?

74

STEVE. I — Okay. So there's — *Look, it's not even my joke, okay?!!*
It was told to me by Kyle Hendrickson, who, for what it's worth,
happens to be —
LENA. Black.
STEVE. Right.
LENA. So the white man goes to jail.
LINDSEY. *(To Steve.) I can't believe you actually intend to —* !! Fine.
STEVE. Anyway.
LINDSEY. Knock 'em dead.
STEVE. Goes to jail for … you know. Embezzlement. Something.
Little white guy. And he's put in a jail cell with this … uhhh …
LENA. With a black man.
STEVE. Big black guy.
LINDSEY. *(Appalled.)* And why "*big*"? —
STEVE. *(Overlapping, to Lindsey.)* I am repeating, *verbatim*, a joke —
LINDSEY. *(Continuous.)* Why does it have to be "big"? What does
that reveal about your subconscious?
STEVE. *(Conitinuous.)* — in the precise manner in which it was
told to *me*.
LENA. Little white man.
LINDSEY. *(Head in hands.)* Oh god.
LENA. Big black man.
STEVE. In the … yeah, so they … um, slam the cell door … behind
him, I guess, and the black guy turns to the white guy, black guy goes,
"Okay, I'm gonna give you a choice. While you're in here with me,
you can either be the mommy, or you can be the daddy." And the
white guy thinks for a second and he goes, "Uh, well, um, I guess, if
it's up to *me*, then, I guess I'd have to say *I'd* prefer to be the daddy."
(Clears his throat.) And, the black guy goes, "Okay, well then bend
over 'Cuz Mommy's gonna fuck you in the ass." *(Long pause. No one
laughs or smiles. They simply nod or shake their heads. Finally …)*
KATHY. That's not the one I was thinking of.
STEVE. *(Academically.)* So: Is that "*offensive*"?

LENA.	LINDSEY.
No.	*Are you insane??!!!!*

STEVE. *(To Lindsey.)* To *you*. How is it offensive to *you*?
LINDSEY. I don't think it's *me* you should be *asking*.
LENA. No, the problem with *that* joke, see, is that it's not *funny*.
LINDSEY. No shit.
STEVE. *(To Lindsey.) You laughed when I told it to you!!*

LENA. And had it been a *funny* joke —

STEVE. It *is* funny. Yes it is. And and and and the *reason* it's funny, is, is, is that it plays upon certain latent fears of — of — of — of white people, vis-à-vis the —

TOM. Okay. I'd like to add: I'm *gay*.

STEVE.	KATHY.	LINDSEY.
I — I —	See? You never	Nice. Nice
I — I — well, I	know. You really	going, Steven.
didn't know that.	don't. *(To Tom.)*	Nice work.
	I couldn't tell at all.	

TOM. *(To Steve.)* So I guess you think sex *between men* is funny?

STEVE. *Oh, come on!!!*

TOM. Just *inherently* funny.

STEVE. And it's not even *sex*, it's *rape*!

LINDSEY. So *rape* is funny.

STEVE. N — *Yes!!!* In the context of the *joke*.

KATHY. My sister was raped.

STEVE. I quit.

KATHY. So it's offensive to *me*.

LINDSEY. *And* me!

STEVE. *(Re: Tom.) And* him. *And* them. *That's the point of the joke.* To permit the expression of — And what does it even *mean*, "offended"? I don't even know what it *means*.

KEVIN. How many white men does it take to change a light bulb?

TOM.	LINDSEY.	KATHY.	STEVE.
Okay, I'm	No. Can we	Aha. See?	*Fine!* Tell me
about two	*not*? I'm asking	Shoe's on	the joke. I
minutes from	you as a favor.	the other	want to hear
leaving? So,		foot now.	it. I do. How
heads up.			many white men
			does it take to
			change a light bulb?

KEVIN. All of 'em.

STEVE. And why is that?

KEVIN. One to hold the light bulb while the rest of 'em screw the entire world.

STEVE.	KATHY.	TOM.	LINDSEY.
So?!! You think I'm	I like that one.	Uhh, if I	Okay, stop.
"*offended*"? I can	I'm telling my	may beg to	Everybody just
do this all day.	husband that.	differ?	*stop*.

76

STEVE. *(Continuous.)* What's long and hard on a black man?

LINDSEY. *How is this happening?!!*

KEVIN. I don't know, Steve. What *is* long and hard on a black man?

STEVE. First grade. Are you "offended"?

KEVIN. Nope.

STEVE. Neither am I.

LINDSEY. You *can't be* offended, you *moron* —

STEVE. *(Astonished laugh.)* … I *can't*?

LINDSEY. *(Continuous.)* — because you've *never* been politically marginalized, unlike *the majority* of people in the world —

STEVE. *(Overlapping.)* How can a *majority* be *marginal*?

LINDSEY. *(Continuous.)* — and, by the way, *all women, everywhere,* and it's your classic white male myopia that you're blind to that basic fact.

LENA. Why is a white woman like a tampon? *(All turn to Lena. Pause.)*

LINDSEY. Why is what?

LENA. It's a joke.

KEVIN. *(To Lena.)* No no no no no no —

LENA. *You* told a joke, now *I'm* telling one: why is a white woman —

KEVIN. *(Overlapping.)* Baby, don't.

LENA. *(Calmly, continuous to Kevin.)* — and please don't *baby* me. You've got three babies at *home* —

KEVIN. *(Publicly, overlapping.)* Good night. I wash my hands.

LENA. *(Continuous, privately.)* — if you need to *pacify* someone. *(To the others.)* So:

STEVE. *(Raising a finger.)* Uhh … can you repeat the setup?

LENA. Why …

STEVE. … is a white woman, right…?

LENA. … like a tampon? *(Steve looks around. No one else answers, so …)*

STEVE. Um, I don't know, why?

LENA. Because they're both stuck up cunts. *(Pause. Again, no one laughs or smiles. Kevin shakes his head.)*

LINDSEY. *(Even.)* Wow.

LENA. But I hope you're not *offended*.

STEVE. *(Academically, not laughing.)* See, *I* find that funny.

LINDSEY. Do you.

KATHY. Well, *I'm* offended.

STEVE. *Oh, you are not.*

LINDSEY. And how does it always comes back around to *the women*?

LENA. *(Innocently.)* It was just a joke.

STEVE. *Exactly!!*

KATHY. An extremely *hostile* joke.

LINDSEY. Directed at me.

KATHY. And in what way am I *stuck-up*, exactly? You mean, because I worked my ass off putting myself through law school, that makes me *stuck-up*?

STEVE. It's a joke about a *tampon*!!

KATHY. And maybe there's a difference between being *stuck up* and being *intelligent*.

STEVE. *(To Kathy.) You don't even know the fucking capital of Morocco!!!*

KATHY. *(Insulted.)* Ohhhhhhh … kay.

STEVE. And you know something? If there's anyone here who's being *marginalized* by the tide of history — You don't exactly see *me* sitting in the White House, do you?

LINDSEY. *Thank the lord.*

STEVE. But you don't see *me* wetting my pants and acting all "offended."

KATHY. *(To Lindsey, as she packs her things.)* You know, I think maybe I'm *done*.

STEVE. No. You want to know what offends *me*? How about the neighborhood the two of us are living in right now? Bunch of white suburban assholes still driving around with the yellow ribbon magnets on their SUVs in support of some bullshit war. *That's* the kinda shit that offends *me*.

KEVIN. Why does *that* make them assholes?

STEVE. *(Beat.)* Why does what?

KEVIN. Said assholes have yellow ribbons on their SU —

STEVE. I didn't say that.

KEVIN. Yeah, you did, you said —

STEVE. I said "*with*" the magnet, not, you know, "*by virtue of.*"

KEVIN. So, it's not the *magnet* makes you the asshole?

LINDSEY. *(To Kevin.)* You have one on your car?

KEVIN. I have three of 'em.

STEVE. Three.

KEVIN. Three.

LINDSEY. Three?

LENA. Three.

STEVE. Three.

KEVIN. One for each member of my family serving overseas.

STEVE. Great. *(Beat.)*

KATHY. *(To Steve.)* I have the pink one for breast cancer.

KEVIN. So maybe I'm a *triple* asshole, but —

LINDSEY. *(Fake whisper to Kevin.) I think we know who the asshole is.*

STEVE. Wow.

LINDSEY. *(Finishing off Steve.)* Well you're being an *idiot*. And in case you hadn't noticed, the rest of the world has begun a more sophisticated conversation about this topic than you apparently are qualified to participate in at this incredible moment in history. I mean, I used to *date* a black guy. *So what?* I mean, *seriously. Steve. Wake up. (The same church bell that we heard in Act One begins to ring. Pause. Tom looks at his watch.)*

TOM. *(Claps hands together.)* And it is now four o'clock.

STEVE. *(Privately, to Lindsey.)* When did you date a black guy?

TOM. So: Final thoughts? Lena?

LENA. No.

TOM. Kev?

KEVIN. I'm good.

TOM. Anybody?

KEVIN. Very informative.

LINDSEY. Well, I want to say this: I want to say I feel angry. And I'm basically kind of hurt by the implication that's been made that, just because we want to live as your neighbors and raise a child alongside yours, that somehow, in the process of doing that, we've had our ethics called into question. Because *that* is hurtful.

LENA. *(Calmly.)* No one has questioned your *ethics* at all.

LINDSEY. Well, I wish I could believe you.

LENA. No, what we're questioning is your *taste. (The others start to leave.)*

TOM.	LINDSEY.
Kathy? I will call you when the petition goes through.	Well, *that* was insulting.

KATHY. Thank you.

TOM. Tuesday at the latest.

LINDSEY. Wait, what's wrong with our *taste?*

TOM. *(Putting on sunglasses.)* Kev?

KEVIN. Right behind you.

LINDSEY. No. What is so *egregious* about the design of our *house?*

KEVIN. *(To Lena, who is about to respond.)* No no no no no. Let it go. *(Lena exits.)*

KATHY. *(To Lindsey.)* Sweetie, I've got a thing but I'll call you tomorrow.

TOM. *(To Lindsey and Steve.)* And you guys got my number if you want to talk?

STEVE. Yep. *(Tom is gone, with a thumbs-up. Kathy follows close behind. At the same time, Dan enters from the kitchen carrying a pair of bolt cutters. The others ignore him.)*

KEVIN. *(To Lindsey and Steve.)* So, uhh … good luck with your house. And maybe y'all can just communicate with Tom from here on out. But, anyway, uhh … *(With a wave.)* y'all enjoy the rest of your evening. *(Kevin politely exits through the open front door. Steve and Lindsey stand silently for a moment, then:)*

DAN. *(Holding up the bolt cutters.)* Uhhhhh…?

LINDSEY. *(Quietly.)* Wow.

STEVE. Wow is right.

LINDSEY. Amazing.

STEVE. *(But not quietly enough.)* And for the record? *That woman is the cunt.* *(And instantly Kevin is back through the front door.)*

KEVIN. *(Advancing on Steve.)* Wait a second — *what'd* you say? *(All hell breaks loose.)*

LENA.	KEVIN.	STEVE.	LINDSEY.
(Following Kevin.) Just leave it alone. Let 'em be. I don't care what kinda bullshit they think, all I want to do is go home now and take the longest shower of my life.	Whattya think I'm *deaf* or something? Standing right there on your front doorstep — Oh no, I *heard* you loud and clear. I'm just giving you the opportunity to repeat it to my *face* —	*(Innocently.)* What? What? What? Hey, hey, *whoa.* *Back off,* man. What is your fucking problem, dude? I didn't do anything to you *or* to her so why can't you *chill?*	*(To Kevin.)* No no no — I told you. It's the pressure. We're both under a huge amount of pressure and yes he acted like an idiot but could we all just maybe *step off,* please?

KEVIN. *(Continuous, in the clear.)* — and when you do? I will slap the taste outa your mouth.

STEVE. | LENA.

STEVE.
Oh oh oh good, *threaten me.*

LENA.
(To Kevin.) Oh, *now* you're gonna stand up for me?

KEVIN. Don't you ever insult my wife, you hear me, *bitch*?

DAN. *(Putting his hand on Kevin's shoulder.)* Hey. Let's be civilized.

KEVIN. *(Whirling on Dan.)* Ohoho, don't you touch *me.*

DAN.
Whoa whoa whoa. That's cool. I'm just passing through, is all.

STEVE.
(To Dan.) Hey, do you *mind*, okay? We happen to be having a conversation.

KEVIN.
(To Dan.) Go putting your hands on *me*? Oh, no. Not in *this* neighbor —

LENA.
(To Kevin.) Oh, for god's sake, are you coming —

LENA. *(Continuous.)* — or are you too busy trying to make *friends* with everybody? *(Dan backs off as two simultaneous arguments unfold.)*

LINDSEY.
(To Steve.) And why the fuck did you go and insult Kathy? We are *paying her*, I hope you you realize?

STEVE.
Yeah, well you know what? I *agree* with them! *The house is too fucking big!*

LINDSEY. Ohhhhhhhh do not *even* —

STEVE.
Very first time we saw the plans. What did I tell you? I told you that like *fifteen times*!! —

LINDSEY.
Well, Steven, you're free to live wherever you want, but the baby and I will be here if you ever feel like visiting.

STEVE.
Fine by me.

LINDSEY. Do you have the keys?

KEVIN.
(To Lena.) What the hell is that supposed to — ?

LENA.
Alllllllll afternoon. Always gotta be *everybody's* friend. *Hi every-body! I'm Kevin!*

KEVIN. *(Starting to exit.)*
Oh gimme a fuckin' — So you want to fight with *me* now? Gotta pick a fight with *me*? You have had a bug up your ass from the moment we walked through this door.

LENA.
Yeah, well maybe some of us don't feel the need to constantly *ingratiate* ourselves with everybody.

KEVIN.
Well, maybe that's because some of us aren't *paranoid and delusional. (Kevin and Lena exit. By this point, Dan has succeeded in opening the trunk.)*

STEVE. I mean, god forbid my needs should ever come before the *baby's*.

LINDSEY. You really want me to choose between you and the baby?

STEVE. Oh, I'm secondary.

LINDSEY. 'Cuz that's an *easy* one.

STEVE. Correction: *tertiary. (As Lindsey and Steve continue to argue, a bespectacled young man in a military uniform descends the stairs, unnoticed and oddly out of place. This is Kenneth, played by the actor who played Tom. He carries a yellow legal pad and a transistor radio. Oblivious to the scene around him, he takes a seat by a window near the front door. As Dan removes a yellowed envelope from the trunk. Lindsey and Steve prepare to leave as the bickering continues uninterrupted.)*

LINDSEY. Or maybe you don't *want* the baby.

STEVE. Oh! That's funny. I didn't know I had a *choice.*

LINDSEY. Oh, you had a choice.

STEVE. If only I'd *known.*

LINDSEY. And you *chose.*

STEVE. And what were the options, again? Oh that's right. A.) *Let's have a baby.*

LINDSEY. Which you *chose.*

STEVE. Or B.) *I'm divorcing you.*

LINDSEY. But *you* chose A.

STEVE. A for Arm-twisting.

LINDSEY. Do you have the keys?

STEVE. B for *Blackmail.*

LINDSEY. *(From outside.) Do* you have them or don't — ?

STEVE. *(From the door.) YES! YES I HAVE THE GODDAMN —* What, you think someone's gonna *rob* this place? *(Dan turns to see them exit.)* Help yourselves. Fuckin' shithole. *(Steve slams the door. Dan looks around with no acknowledgment of Kenneth.)*

DAN. *(To the empty house.)* Hello? *(He waits for a reply.)* Hello? *(He sits on the trunk, opens the letter. Reading to himself.)* Dear Mom and Dad. *(Lights change. Kenneth switches on the transistor radio and music begins to play, not unlike the very beginning of the play. It is early morning, 1957. Dim light filters through the window, barely illuminating Kenneth. He bends over his legal pad, writing, as Bev slowly descends the stairs, dressed in her robe and slippers. She stops near the bottom.)*

BEV. *(Bleary-eyed, confused.)* Kenneth? *(Kenneth turns down the volume on the radio.)*

KENNETH. Hmm?

BEV. What are you doing down here?

KENNETH. Writing a letter.

BEV. Did your father leave already?

KENNETH. *(Looks outside.)* I don't see the car.

BEV. What time is it?

KENNETH. Don't know.

BEV. I overslept.

KENNETH. Yup.

BEV. *(Yawning.)* I don't know why I was up so late. I was up half the night and the house was so quiet and your father was sound asleep but for some reason my mind was just racing and it took forever to fall asleep.

KENNETH. Go back to bed.

BEV. *(Finally focusing.)* Oh, look how you're dressed up. Why are you all dressed up like that? *(Kenneth stares, doesn't answer.)* Kenneth?

KENNETH. Job interview. *(A key turns in the front door. It opens and Francine enters in her street clothes with a scarf tied around her head. She carries a wet umbrella.)*

FRANCINE. *(Sleepy.)* Morning.

KENNETH. Morning.

BEV. Morning, Francine.

FRANCINE. Morning.

BEV. Oh, is it *raining* out there?

FRANCINE. Sprinkling a little.

BEV. I didn't even notice. Well. It's good for the grass. *(She stands at the bottom of the stairs, as Francine crosses past her and up the hallway. Bev hesitates.)*

KENNETH. Aren't you going back to sleep?

BEV. *(Pensive.)* Oh, I will. I'm just about to. *(For a moment, she stares into space, then turns to Kenneth, brightly.)* But you know, I think things are about to change. I really do. I know it's been a hard couple of years for all of us, I know they have been, but I really believe things are about to change for the better. I firmly believe that. *(Kenneth waits. Bev turns and starts back up the stairs.)* You have enough light, there?

KENNETH. Uh-huh.

BEV. *(As she ascends.)* Well, don't hurt your eyes. *(She is gone. Kenneth turns the radio back up, resumes writing. Dan continues to read. The lights slowly fade as the music concludes.)*

End of Play

AUTHOR'S NOTE

This is the script of the play as it was performed in New York and beyond. Now, however, after hearing it hundreds of times, my preference would be to alter the final scene — which was written in the original partly to accommodate costume changes — in the following way, with a deletion in one of Bev's lines. The adjusted version would read ...

BEV. *(Bleary-eyed, confused.)* Kenneth? *(Kenneth turns down the volume on the radio.)*
KENNETH. Hmm?
BEV. What are you doing down here?
KENNETH. Writing a letter.
BEV. Did your father leave already?
KENNETH. *(Looks outside.)* I don't see the car.
BEV. What time is it?
KENNETH. Don't know.
BEV. I overslept.
KENNETH. Yup.
BEV. *(Yawning.)* I don't know why I was up so late.
KENNETH. Go back to bed.
BEV. *(Noticing Kenneth's uniform.)* Oh, look how you're dressed up. Why are you all dressed up like that? *(Kenneth stares, doesn't answer.)* Kenneth?
KENNETH. Job interview.

... and it would continue as written until the end of the play. But if the actress playing Francine can't make the costume change, the choice is up to you.

PROPERTY LIST

Cardboard boxes
National Geographic magazine
Carton of ice cream
Spoon
Radio
Linens
Chafing dish
Packing materials
Large shovel
Glasses of iced tea
Pad, pencil
Large green padlocked Army footlocker, with envelope containing
    letter on yellow legal paper
Aged versions of same footlocker (covered in mold and dirt) and
    letter (in yellowed envelope)
Earrings
2 bags with hand-me-downs
Purse
Tissue or handkerchief
Men's work gloves
Iced drinks
Xeroxed documents
2 cell phones
Chewing gum
Bolt cutters
Yellow legal pad, pen
Transistor radio
Wet umbrella

SOUND EFFECTS

Music from radio
Landline phone ring
Doorbell
Church bell
Cell phone ring
Truck horn

NEW PLAYS

★ **ACT ONE by James Lapine.** Growing up in an impoverished Bronx family and forced to drop out of school at age thirteen, Moss Hart dreamed of joining the glamorous world of the theater. Hart's famous memoir *Act One* plots his unlikely collaboration with the legendary playwright George S. Kaufman and his arrival on Broadway. Tony Award-winning writer and director James Lapine has adapted Act One for the stage, creating a funny, heartbreaking and suspenseful celebration of a playwright and his work. "…brims contagiously with the ineffable, irrational and irrefutable passion for that endangered religion called the Theater." –NY Times. "…wrought with abundant skill and empathy." –Time Out. [8M, 4W] ISBN: 978-0-8222-3217-9

★ **THE VEIL by Conor McPherson.** May 1822, rural Ireland. The defrocked Reverend Berkeley arrives at the crumbling former glory of Mount Prospect House to accompany a young woman to England. Seventeen-year-old Hannah is to be married off to a marquis in order to resolve the debts of her mother's estate. However, compelled by the strange voices that haunt his beautiful young charge and a fascination with the psychic current that pervades the house, Berkeley proposes a séance, the consequences of which are catastrophic. "…an effective mixture of dark comedy and suspense." –Telegraph (London). "A cracking fireside tale of haunting and decay." –Times (London). [3M, 5W] ISBN: 978-0-8222-3313-8

★ **AN OCTOROON by Branden Jacobs-Jenkins. Winner of the 2014 OBIE Award for Best New American Play.** Judge Peyton is dead and his plantation Terrebonne is in financial ruins. Peyton's handsome nephew George arrives as heir apparent and quickly falls in love with Zoe, a beautiful octoroon. But the evil overseer M'Closky has other plans—for both Terrebonne and Zoe. In 1859, a famous Irishman wrote this play about slavery in America. Now an American tries to write his own. "AN OCTOROON invites us to laugh loudly and easily at how naïve the old stereotypes now seem, until nothing seems funny at all." –NY Times [10M, 5W] ISBN: 978-0-8222-3226-1

★ **IVANOV translated and adapted by Curt Columbus.** In this fascinating early work by Anton Chekhov, we see the union of humor and pathos that would become his trademark. A restless man, Nicholai Ivanov struggles to dig himself out of debt and out of provincial boredom. When the local doctor, Lvov, informs Ivanov that his wife Anna is dying and accuses him of worsening her condition with his foul moods, Ivanov is sent into a downward spiral of depression and ennui. He soon finds himself drawn to a beautiful young woman, Sasha, full of hope and energy. Finding himself stuck between a romantic young mistress and his ailing wife, Ivanov falls deeper into crisis, heading toward inevitable tragedy. [8M, 8W] ISBN: 978-0-8222-3155-4

DRAMATISTS PLAY SERVICE, INC.
440 Park Avenue South, New York, NY 10016 212-683-8960 Fax 212-213-1539
postmaster@dramatists.com www.dramatists.com

NEW PLAYS

★ **I'LL EAT YOU LAST: A CHAT WITH SUE MENGERS by John Logan.** For more than 20 years, Sue Mengers' clients were the biggest names in show business: Barbra Streisand, Faye Dunaway, Burt Reynolds, Ali MacGraw, Gene Hackman, Cher, Candice Bergen, Ryan O'Neal, Nick Nolte, Mike Nichols, Gore Vidal, Bob Fosse…If her clients were the talk of the town, she was the town, and her dinner parties were the envy of Hollywood. Now, you're invited into her glamorous Beverly Hills home for an evening of dish, dirty secrets and all the inside showbiz details only Sue can tell you. "A delectable soufflé of a solo show…thanks to the buoyant, witty writing of Mr. Logan" –NY Times. "80 irresistible minutes of primo tinseltown dish from a certified master chef." –Hollywood Reporter. [1W] ISBN: 978-0-8222-3079-3

★ **PUNK ROCK by Simon Stephens.** In a private school outside of Manchester, England, a group of highly-articulate seventeen-year-olds flirt and posture their way through the day while preparing for their A-Level mock exams. With hormones raging and minimal adult supervision, the students must prepare for their future — and survive the savagery of high school. Inspired by playwright Simon Stephens' own experiences as a teacher, PUNK ROCK is an honest and unnerving chronicle of contemporary adolescence. "[A] tender, ferocious and frightning play." –NY Times. "[A] muscular little play that starts out funny and ferocious then reveals its compassion by degrees." –Hollywood Reporter. [5M, 3W] ISBN: 978-0-8222-3288-9

★ **THE COUNTRY HOUSE by Donald Margulies.** A brood of famous and longing-to-be-famous creative artists have gathered at their summer home during the Williamstown Theatre Festival. When the weekend takes an unexpected turn, everyone is forced to improvise, inciting a series of simmering jealousies, romantic outbursts, and passionate soul-searching. Both witty and compelling, THE COUNTRY HOUSE provides a piercing look at a family of performers coming to terms with the roles they play in each other's lives. "A valentine to the artists of the stage." –NY Times. "Remarkably candid and funny." –Variety. [3M, 3W] ISBN: 978-0-8222-3274-2

★ **OUR LADY OF KIBEHO by Katori Hall.** Based on real events, OUR LADY OF KIBEHO is an exploration of faith, doubt, and the power and consequences of both. In 1981, a village girl in Rwanda claims to see the Virgin Mary. Ostracized by her schoolmates and labeled disturbed, everyone refuses to believe, until impossible happenings appear again and again. Skepticism gives way to fear, and then to belief, causing upheaval in the school community and beyond. "Transfixing." –NY Times. "Hall's passionate play renews belief in what theater can do." –Time Out [7M, 8W, 1 boy] ISBN: 978-0-8222-3301-5

DRAMATISTS PLAY SERVICE, INC.
440 Park Avenue South, New York, NY 10016 212-683-8960 Fax 212-213-1539
postmaster@dramatists.com www.dramatists.com

NEW PLAYS

★ **AGES OF THE MOON by Sam Shepard.** Byron and Ames are old friends, reunited by mutual desperation. Over bourbon on ice, they sit, reflect and bicker until fifty years of love, friendship and rivalry are put to the test at the barrel of a gun. "A poignant and honest continuation of themes that have always been present in the work of one of this country's most important dramatists, here reconsidered in the light and shadow of time passed." –NY Times. "Finely wrought...as enjoyable and enlightening as a night spent stargazing." –Talkin' Broadway. [2M] ISBN: 978-0-8222-2462-4

★ **ALL THE WAY by Robert Schenkkan. Winner of the 2014 Tony Award for Best Play.** November, 1963. An assassin's bullet catapults Lyndon Baines Johnson into the presidency. A Shakespearean figure of towering ambition and appetite, this charismatic, conflicted Texan hurls himself into the passage of the Civil Rights Act—a tinderbox issue emblematic of a divided America—even as he campaigns for re-election in his own right, and the recognition he so desperately wants. In Pulitzer Prize and Tony Award–winning Robert Schenkkan's vivid dramatization of LBJ's first year in office, means versus ends plays out on the precipice of modern America. ALL THE WAY is a searing, enthralling exploration of the morality of power. It's not personal, it's just politics. "...action-packed, thoroughly gripping... jaw-dropping political drama." –Variety. "A theatrical coup...nonstop action. The suspense of a first-class thriller." –NY1. [17M, 3W] ISBN: 978-0-8222-3181-3

★ **CHOIR BOY by Tarell Alvin McCraney.** The Charles R. Drew Prep School for Boys is dedicated to the creation of strong, ethical black men. Pharus wants nothing more than to take his rightful place as leader of the school's legendary gospel choir. Can he find his way inside the hallowed halls of this institution if he sings in his own key? "[An] affecting and honest portrait...of a gay youth tentatively beginning to find the courage to let the truth about himself become known." –NY Times. "In his stirring and stylishly told drama, Tarell Alvin McCraney cannily explores race and sexuality and the graces and gravity of history." –NY Daily News. [7M] ISBN: 978-0-8222-3116-5

★ **THE ELECTRIC BABY by Stefanie Zadravec.** When Helen causes a car accident that kills a young man, a group of fractured souls cross paths and connect around a mysterious dying baby who glows like the moon. Folk tales and folklore weave throughout this magical story of sad endings, strange beginnings and the unlikely people that get you from one place to the next. "The imperceptible magic that pervades human existence and the power of myth to assuage sorrow are invoked by the playwright as she entwines the lives of strangers in THE ELECTRIC BABY, a touching drama." –NY Times. "As dazzling as the dialogue is dreamful." –Pittsburgh City Paper. [3M, 3W] ISBN: 978-0-8222-3011-3

DRAMATISTS PLAY SERVICE, INC.
440 Park Avenue South, New York, NY 10016 212-683-8960 Fax 212-213-1539
postmaster@dramatists.com www.dramatists.com